THE RELUCTANT ALLIANCE

Behaviorism and Humanism

BOBBY NEWMAN

PROMETHEUS BOOKS • BUFFALO, NEW YORK

Published 1992 by Prometheus Books

96 95 94 93 92   5 4 3 2 1

Library of Congress Cataloging-in-Publication Data

Newman, Bobby.
    The reluctant alliance : behaviorism and humanism / by Bobby Newman.
        p.   cm.
    Includes bibliographical references.
    ISBN 0-087975-727-2 (alk. paper)
    1. Humanism. 2. Behaviorism (Psychology). 3. Humanistic ethics.
4. Behavior modification—Moral and ethical aspects. 5. Psychology and philosophy.
6. Social problems. 7. Social control. I. Title.
B821.N46   1992
144—dc20   92-745
                                                                      CIP

Printed in the United States of America on acid-free paper.

This book is dedicated to the memory of Linda Yalem, writer, runner, student, sister, and friend. She loved learning and wanted to realize all the positive in life. Her life, and the manner in which it was taken, reminded us of what is truly important, and how far we have to go in understanding human behavior. Linda will never be forgotten.

Ann Yalem Brown—Linda Yalem's sister
Bobby Newman

Contents

Preface

In the pages that follow I will make the claim that, contrary to popular opinion, humanism and radical behaviorism (the philosophical framework of applied behavior analysis) are complementary systems of thought. I will do this by tracing historical developments, stated philosophies and intentions, and research findings.

Following the example of some of the more enthusiastic thinkers whose work I describe, I give the reader the credit of knowing that what I say is my opinion. As such, I do not begin many sentences with "I think," or "I believe," or "It seems to me." Because of this, many of the statements may appear more definite and absolute than the evidence would seem to allow. This is to avoid clumsy ambivalences, and not to suggest that I believe my analysis is unquestionably correct. I have presented samples of the research that led me to arrive at the conclusions stated.

Also, because this is not a work devoted exclusively to history, the historical treatments are necessarily brief and omit many facts and individuals that would be key to an exhaustive analysis. Again, things may seem much more definite than they actually are. Past experiences constantly influence the future in subtle ways, and thus to say that one period began or ended at a specific time, or that

9

one practice was present in one era and not in another, is nearly impossible. It is probably true that many practices and ideas that are particularly identified with one era were also present in other eras. For the sake of providing a picture that allows identifiable transitions, I have ignored many such blurred lines. It is my intention to provide a readable background for the layperson. The experts in the history of humanism or applied behavior analysis should skip these sections, for they would probably regard them as inadequate.

Little of what I present will be original to this text. I do hope, however, that I can update the discussion and that my own perspective and experiences will add to the existing literature. The main ideas have been discussed by many writers (e.g., Hawkins 1985, MacCorquodale 1971, Skinner 1976, Wilson and O'Leary 1980, Woolfolk and Richardson 1980) for some time. I did not deliberately omit anyone, but, because this subject matter has been explored for several years, it is possible that I might have missed important recent scholarship. For this I apologize.

Finally, it is often difficult to discover who originated a particular line of thinking. Many of the thoughts described were well-known before the birth of the individual to whom I give credit. I go along with Stephen Jay Gould (1988), who states that coming up with revolutionary ideas is easy; the impressive act is to find a way to test the idea and prove its veracity. I would add that once this is done, it is equally impressive to popularize ideas and find ways to apply them. As such, I gave credit not necessarily to the originators of ideas, but rather to their testers and popularizers.

I must thank Leo Newman, Nancy Hemmes, and Dawn Buffington for considerable conceptual and editorial assistance. Warm thanks are also extended to Henrietta Newman, Susan Cara, Donald A. Cook, John O. Cooper, John W. Eshleman, and Robert Lanson for helpful comments and encouragement, and to Richard W. Malott for encouragement and the self-management ideas that allowed me to get this project done. Obviously, mention must also be made of B. F. Skinner and his writings, not the least of which being a letter written to a student of behavior analysis one year before his death. Despite his busy schedule, not to mention failing health and problems with his vision, Dr. Skinner took the time to read a paper sent to him by a student he had never heard of, and to offer encouragement and helpful comments.

1

Humanism and Applied Behavior Analysis: An Examination

Two of today's most anxiety-provoking systems of thought are *humanism* and *radical behaviorism,* the latter being the philosophical framework of applied behavior analysis. The anxiety these two systems elicit is traceable to the same source: both humanism and radical behaviorism challenge some of society's most comforting notions, and suggest that old illusions must be cast off and new responsibilities assumed if humanity is to have a chance of survival in this time of global crises (e.g., overpopulation, the greenhouse effect, the threat of nuclear war). Provoking such anxiety, humanism and radical behaviorism are also two of today's most misunderstood and unfairly attacked systems of thought (Madigan 1988, Morris 1984). Ironically, proponents of either one of these viewpoints have rarely accepted the other as valid, and have at times been at polite (and at times not so polite) philosophical war with one another (e.g., Day 1971, Matson 1971). It is my intention to demonstrate that the differences between the two systems are not as great as they are made to seem. More importantly, I will suggest that each system contains flaws that can be corrected by combining elements of the other. I will begin by defining the current forms and describing the histories of both humanism and applied behavior analysis, suggest commonalities and differences and isolate where I believe each system is deficient. Finally, I will suggest how each system's deficiencies can be corrected by incorporating ideas from its rival. In later chapters I will suggest what the systems have to offer one another with regard to psychotherapy, moral and academic education, and public policy.

CONTEMPORARY HUMANISM

Humanism is a difficult philosophy to define. The term has historically been used, and misused, to describe philosophies that contain fundamental and profound differences (e.g., secular versus religious humanism). The humanism I shall be describing when I use the term is "naturalistic humanism," the philosophy described by Corliss Lamont (1982) and one which is compatible with the *Humanist Manifestos I and II* (Kurtz 1973). Humanism, as it is currently conceptualized and as I mean the term, is best described by a statement of its philosophy offered by the American Humanist Association:

> Humanism is optimistic regarding human nature and confident in human reason and science as the best means of reaching the goal of human fulfillment in this world. Humanists affirm that humans are a product of the same evolutionary process that produced all other living organisms and that all ideas, knowledge, values, and social systems are based upon human experience. Humanists conclude that creative ability and personal responsibility are strongest when the mind is free from supernatural belief and operates in an atmosphere of freedom and democracy. [Membership card, American Humanist Association, 1991]

A BRIEF AND ABRIDGED HISTORY OF HUMANISM

As with much Western thought, hints of humanism were present in the thought of the ancient Greeks, most notably in that of the Sophist Protagoras (481?–411 B.C.E.). Protagoras made no secret of his agnosticism, and made the bold pronouncement "Man is the measure of all things" (Guthrie 1986/1956, p. 28). While he probably meant this in a relativistic rather than humanistic sense, it was still a notable step away from the supernatural theories that prevailed among the great thinkers of the time. Even Plato (427?–347? B.C.E.), although he did engage in this-worldly thought, was often tied up in heavy supernaturalism. These ancient thinkers are not to be blamed for their failure to make a complete break from supernaturalism, however. Little of nature was understood at that time, and as such it must have seemed as though there had to be a supernatural force at work behind existence. The break from supernaturalism was to come slowly and had to wait for the emergence of science and naturalism.

It was Aristotle (384–322 B.C.E.), through his development of logic and classification, who provided a coherent picture of science as a method of inquiry. This early scientific method was refined centuries later during the period known as the Renaissance; it would provide the final impetus for the maturation of humanism as a philosophy. Aristotle's own physics and metaphysics, however, remained supernaturalistic, requiring a "prime mover" to begin action and to maintain it. Ironically, this requirement for a deity allowed scholastics such as Thomas Aquinas (1225?–1274) to incorporate Aristotelian philosophy into the thought of the Catholic Church (Frost 1942). The Church came to hold massive power in medieval times, and Aristotelian philosophy was perpetuated through its association with Christianity. Aristotle has thus been used by different individuals for starkly contrasting ends. Aristotle was not alone in having work interpreted as the reader saw fit. Butterfield (1957, p. 123) paraphrases Descartes, "He says in the *Discourse* that when he hears his own views repeated he finds them so changed that he cannot recognize or acknowledge them as his—a remark which must go straight to the heart of every author."

During the Renaissance, the Aristotelian/Christian system came into serious question. The process of recovering the knowledge of antiquity, which had been lost to Westerners during the early Dark Ages (but kept by the Arabs), was slowly coming to an end. The world became gradually aware that systems other than that of Aristotle had been worked out during antiquity, and a desire to settle the newly discovered controversies was born. It was this spirit of questioning that led to new developments in philosophy and science.

It was a rather awkward time. Aristotle's philosophy had been carefully scrutinized, and many of his scientific theories were crumbling (Butterfield 1957). What must be remembered, however, is that most of the scientists and philosophers of the day were pious individuals seeking to service both Church and God. Fortunately or unfortunately, the results of their work ultimately did not conform to their intentions. Nicholas Copernicus (1473–1543), for example, demonstrated that the earth was not the center of the universe, thus casting serious doubts on a literal interpretation of the cosmology found in the Bible. Despite post hoc theories designed to save the old views, it was clear that the old world-view was dissolving and a new one was needed to take its place. Two individuals are especially important in the construction of the new world view, which would evolve into modern science. These individuals were Francis Bacon (1561–1626) and René Descartes (1596–1650) (Butterfield, pp. 108-128).

Bacon had become frustrated by the seemingly irresolvable nature of the philosophic debates. The merging of the Aristotelian and Christian world-views had left several annoying questions, particularly as the system began to break down. There was a general call among intellectuals for a revolution to answer the questions of the day posed by philosophers, theologians, and scientists (e.g., Robinson 1986):

1. Are the heavenly bodies made of some incorruptible substance?

2. What is the nature of the Aristotelian "final cause"?

3. Should such causes be included in physics or metaphysics?

4. Are there any unquestionable truths to guide us?

5. Can logic or revelation answer all the questions of existence, or should experiments and observation form the basis of our knowledge?

Bacon favored and popularized the idea of the scientific method, calling for experiments to be performed in a systematic fashion in order to arrive at indisputably correct answers to the questions of material existence ("putting nature to the question," to use a rather chilling metaphor). The metaphysical questions were left to the theologians and philosophers (e.g., Butterfield 1957, p. 117: "The very highest generalizations of all, however, are out of reach, too near to God and to final causes; they must be left to the philosopher.").

Descartes advocated a different view of science. He suggested that deduction from unquestionable facts (e.g., God's perfection) would lead to the truth not only about nature, but also about all of existence and of God. Using deductive methods, experiments when necessary, and especially mathematics, Descartes formulated the modern law of inertia and opened the door to the mechanistic physics of Isaac Newton (1642–1727).

With the establishment of Newtonian physics, the need for a deity waned, and the picture of God created by the mingling of Aristotelian metaphysics and Christian theology became less plausible. A new viewpoint thus evolved, Deism (Lamont 1982, p. 55):

> The viewpoint of Deism was essentially that God created the Universe at the beginning of things, and then, retiring to the comfortable status of Deity Emeritus, left the world-machine to work out its own self-evolution according to natural law.

Sherwin Wine (1985, p. 15) captures the gravity of this shift in perspective:

> The Enlightenment kept God for ceremonial purposes but castrated him. By the time we get to Newton and Voltaire, he has been retired from active duty. He is only allowed to design and manufacture the world. Once the laws of nature are in place, he cannot even change his mind. He remains a helpless spectator, an unemployed deity, unable to intervene in the affairs of the world. If the gods have nursing homes, he is in one of them.

What we have seen is a gradual shift away from the view of an all-present, all-active deity (Aristotle and medieval Christianity), to a central and necessary philosophical assumption (Descartes), to a contented watcher (Deism). Two final death blows were left to be dealt: disproving the Bible as a document of supernatural origin, and the subsequent questioning of God's existence. This effort, begun earlier (perhaps unwittingly) by individuals such as Copernicus, was completed in the nineteenth and twentieth centuries. The work of such individuals as Baron Georges Cuvier (1769–1832) and Sir Charles Lyell (1797–1875) provided the necessary background for Charles Darwin (1809–1882) to present his theory of evolution by natural selection in 1859. The formers' work had discredited Bishop James Usher's notion of a 6,000-year-old Earth. Now, with the theory of evolution, also gone were the biblical notions of fixed species; a chain of being culminating in humanity and then God; and, when combined with the other inaccuracies discovered by science, the notion of the Bible as a historical document to be read literally and used as a guide for living. With the Bible no longer considered literally true, it was necessary to once again rethink philosophic positions. Since the collapse of the medieval world-view, supernatural authority had been losing its influence. Natural authority gradually began to take its place. Auguste Comte (1798–1857) followed this trend to a paradoxical extreme, creating a "positivistic church" that attempted to deny all metaphysical notions. His creation was laden with rituals and has been called Catholicism without Christianity, but it probably provided a necessary link to the less extreme and less ritualized humanism of today.

From this point, shaped by events of the late nineteenth and twentieth centuries, the literature that began with the earliest shifts in world-view, and especially the advance of physical science and anthropology, naturalistic humanism evolved as a philosophy free of supernatural metaphysics. Humanism recognizes no revelation other than that of humanity's scientific inquiries. It is a philosophy born of science and, as if to return the favor, provides the framework from which science should be applied if it is to benefit humankind. It is a democratic philosophy, and one which respects the abilities and rights of human beings to be paramount.

CURRENT APPLIED BEHAVIOR ANALYSIS

Applied behavior analysis is the branch of psychology that seeks to discover and apply the basic principles of behavior acquisition and maintenance (Cooper, Heron, and Heward 1987, p. 15):

> Applied behavior analysis is the science in which procedures derived from the principles of behavior are systematically applied to improve socially significant behavior to a meaningful degree and to demonstrate experimentally that the procedures employed were responsible for the improvement in behavior.

A natural science approach to understanding behavior is used in conducting such an analysis. Behavior is conceptualized in terms of stimuli Antecedent to behavior, the Behavior itself, and the Consequences of behavior (the ABCs of behavior). Functional relationships between environmental stimuli and behavior are the end-products of the discipline.

Being a branch of natural science rather than a philosophy, the term "applied behavior analysis" has been used more consistently than the term "humanism." Confusion has not been totally eliminated, however. Terms such as "applied behavior analysis," "behavior modification," and "behavioral engineering" have been indiscriminately used to refer to any behavior-change procedure. Electroconvulsive therapy, psychosurgery, and drug therapies, for example, have all been associated *incorrectly* with applied behavior analysis. Behavior analysis relies on systematic manipulations of environmental stimuli and is not connected with these radical and exotic procedures. Because it captures the goals and essence of the approach, I shall use "applied behavior analysis," or simply "behavior analysis," to refer to this system.

A second problem is that many who are not trained in the discipline nonetheless consider themselves to be experts. There is no legal control on professional titles related to behavior analysis, and thus many who seek to improve their professional status may claim expertise in this area. They employ procedures based upon a faulty or incomplete understanding of applied behavior analysis: ". . . the approach has an apparent simplicity that can be deceptive and many alluring features that can be misleading" (Bijou 1970).

Consider difficulties associated with extinction procedures. When a behavior is no longer reinforced (positively or negatively), an extinction procedure, it typically gets worse before it gets better. An "extinction burst" is seen, wherein the intensity or rate of the behavior will temporarily increase before decreasing. Suppose, for example, that an individual is trying to eliminate another person's self-injurious behavior by using an extinction procedure. If the trainer does not know about the extinction burst, he or she may become unsettled by the temporary increase in the severity of the self-injury (e.g., a change from head-banging with a hand to head-slamming against the floor or a table) and call an end to the extinction procedure. This misinformed use of behavioral technology has resulted in the creation and reinforcement of a new, much more severe behavior problem. This use of the powerful procedures of behavior analysis by the untrained can lead to serious problems, not to mention credibility problems for the profession.

A Brief and Abridged History of Applied Behavior Analysis

The roots of behavior analysis also go back to ancient Greece and the philosopher/scientist Aristotle. It was he who formulated the rules of mental association that would play such a powerful role in the discipline. Later, the work of the British associationists (Thomas Hobbes, John Locke, James Mill, John Stuart Mill, and Thomas Browne) built on the Aristotelian ideas and suggested that the association of sensory experiences, which followed Aristotle's laws, were responsible for all thought and behavior (Hearst 1988).

In addition to Aristotle's ideas of association, another line of inquiry was to be instrumental in the development of behavior analysis. This second line of inquiry was environmental determinism, the idea that behavior is a result of environmental forces acting lawfully on the organism. We again return to a figure from the history of humanism, Descartes. As legend has it, he was struck by the importance of the concept of the reflex while walking in the gardens of France. These gardens were designed in such a way that when certain stones were depressed, a hydraulic system was activated that moved massive statues toward or away from the visitor. Descartes suggested that perhaps a similar mechanistic system could be responsible for movement in living animals (Catania 1984). The philosophy of Descartes, therefore, was *dualistic* in nature. The mind was free, but the body was constrained by natural law and subject to environmental determinism by way of the reflex. (To what extent Descartes's ideas regarding the mind were shaped by the threat of a disapproving church is unknowable. It is possible that his ideas on the mind were more mechanistic than he let on [see *Le Monde*, published only after the safety of death (Stagner 1988)]). Animals, having no mind in the Cartesian system, were entirely mechanistic with respect to their behavior. Research regarding animal behavior and physiology came to be very important in the development of behavior analysis. This is an important point, that applied behavior analysis does take into account biological influences. The predominant concentration on environmental influences is merely a result of their easier systematic manipulation.

From the mind-body dualism of Descartes, it was but a small step to reject the special status given to mental activity and to assert that both mind and body are subject to environmental determinism. This position was adopted by radical philosopher Julian Offray de La Mettrie (1709–1751) (Kendler 1987) and Comte, who advocated applying the scientific study of human behavior, which he called sociology, to achieve social progress. In this, and in his insistence on observable relationships as the basis of science, Comte anticipated the behavior analysts. (We will return to Comte in chapter five). An early form of the philosophy of behaviorism, wherein behavior is the subject matter for psychology, thus became feasible. With all of human behavior (including "thought behavior") subject to natural law, it became possible to believe that human behavior might be susceptible to a scientific analysis. The idea of scientifically studying humanity and its behavior is an ancient one (the reader is referred to Leahey [1987] for an excellent historical analysis), but it was only at this point that the effort could be carried out.

This scientific analysis of behavior followed the two lines of associationism and environmental determinism. The associative tradition was brought into the laboratory by Herrmann Ebbinghaus in the late nineteenth century. Using himself as a subject, Ebbinghaus experimentally tested (and often confirmed) the old theories of associative learning and memory. While subsequent research has improved upon Ebbinghaus's findings, many of his results still stand over one hundred years later, an impressive feat for any scientist.

The environmental determinism tradition was carried into the laboratory by individuals such as Jacques Loeb (1859–1924), who used plants to demonstrate that behavior could be conceptualized simply as a matter of environmental forces acting directly on the organism. Another key figure was the Soviet physiologist Ivan Sechenov (1829–1905), who is important in two respects. First, it was he who described how mental activity could be conceptualized as a chain of reflexes (one thought providing the stimulus for the next), providing the method by which thought could follow natural law. Second, his methods for studying reflex behavior had a tremendous influence on another Soviet physiologist, Ivan Pavlov (1849–1936).

Pavlov's work marked a turning point in behavioral research. Up to this point, the environment was seen as acting on the organism in a direct stimulus/response relationship. Pavlov, however, discovered that previously neutral stimuli could take on the behavior-eliciting properties of relevant stimuli by way of a conditioning procedure based upon, among other things, contiguity of presentation (e.g., Pavlov's famous demonstration that, after many pairings, the ticking of a metronome or the sound of a bell could take on the saliva-eliciting properties of meat powder). This discovery opened the door to a new conception of the reflex relationship. No longer was behavior simply a matter of stimuli and direct responses. Now, behavior could be seen not only in terms of stimulus/response pairings, but also in terms of stimulus/stimulus pairings. Arbitrary stimuli could be paired with more naturally relevant stimuli, thus increasing the number of stimuli to which an organism would respond. Associationism and environmental determinism, which before Pavlov had been separate traditions, now came together in the form of classical (also known as Pavlovian or respondent) conditioning.

At roughly the same time that Pavlov was conducting his research, another scientist, Edward Thorndike (1874–1949), was conducting research that also linked associationism and environmental determinism. Pavlov's experiments had shown that two stimuli that were presented together could become linked. Thorndike showed that an association could also be built between a given behavior and a stimulus that was a result of that behavior. In Thorndike's experiments, an organism was placed into a box designed in such a way that a particular response would open a door and allow escape. Once outside, the organism would find food left by Thorndike. On the first few trials, the organism would take quite a while before stumbling across the behavior necessary to perform in order to escape from the box. After several trials, the time that lapsed before the organism would emit the required behavior and escape decreased dramatically. Thorndike called this learning by "trial and error," and formulated the "law of effect" to explain how different consequential stimuli affected learning. Later, this type of learning was expanded upon by noted psychologist B. F. Skinner (see below), and renamed operant (or Skinnerian or instrumental) conditioning. Skinner's work completed the picture for environmental determinism and for applied behavior analysis. Originally, there was only the direct stimulus/response relationship. Then came classical conditioning and the discovery that stimuli could be substituted for one another within this stimulus/response relationship. Finally, with developments in operant conditioning, there was a way in which entirely new responses, not originally in the behavioral repertoire of the organism, could be maintained by providing reinforcing stimuli after the behavior had occurred. When taken together with the innate behavior supplied by heredity, there was no behavior, no matter how complex, that could not be explained, at least theoretically, by environmental forces.

At this point we must step back from the history of behavior analysis and take a look at psychology as it was conducted in the late nineteenth and early twentieth centuries. The subject matter of the discipline, for the most part, was mental activity. The method that was used to study mental phenomena was introspection, wherein an experimental subject would describe what (s)he thought when engaged in the act of self-observation. The subject matter of the science, therefore, was not open to public observation and conceptions regarding the nature of mental activity varied widely.

John B. Watson (1878–1958) was dissatisfied by the subjective nature of this pursuit and the lack of progress he perceived to have resulted from it. It was he who called for psychology to become a completely objective science with observable behavior as its only subject matter. He adopted the name *behaviorism* from the earlier philosophical tradition for this philosophy of the science. Watson adopted many controversial positions, one of which was a belief in environmental determinism (although not as extreme as is usually suggested). Those who disagree with Watson often scornfully quote the following passage (Watson 1970/1924, p. 104):

> Give me a dozen healthy infants, well-formed, and my own specified world to bring them up in and I'll guarantee to take any one at random and train him to become any type of specialist I might select—doctor, lawyer, artist, merchant-chief and, yes, even beggarman and thief, regardless of his talents, penchants, tendencies, abilities, vocation, and race of his ancestors.

What is not usually quoted is the continuation of his thought—

> I am going beyond my facts and I admit it, but so have the advocates of the contrary and they have been doing it for many thousands of years.

What is also not appreciated is the context in which this quote was made. This was the day of "scientific racism," when many prominent scientists used biased measures to suggest the innate inferiority of many national groups (Gould 1981). As described by Stephen Jay Gould, this led to tragic consequences, including forced sterilizations and the American refusal of refugees from war-torn Europe. In this respect, instead of being condemned as a mechanistic manipulator (as he often is), Watson should be lauded as a visionary who saw past the prejudices of his day (and even his own dislike of blacks), as well as its (and our) religious excesses (1970/1924, p. 3):

> . . . to doubt its (the soul's) existence is to become a heretic and once might possibly even have led to the loss of one's head. Even today the man holding a public position dare not question it.

Watson was a fiery popularizer of the idea of behavior as the sole subject matter of psychology. He pushed this idea a little too far and too fast, however, backing himself into corners from which he could not escape. Originally, Watson was content to state that mental activity was outside the realm of scientific analysis. Later he entertained the idea that the experience of having a mind was an illusion created by the central nervous system. Watson's tendency to adopt extreme positions created many problems for him, not the least of which has been his dismissal by subsequent generations who do not understand the context of his statements.

Watson was not as successful as he had hoped to be in reforming psychology. There were many factors that led to this failure, including an early exit from academic life, a tendency to adopt extremist positions, and a reliance on Pavlov's paradigm while neglecting Thorndike's. Watson was extremely successful, however, in that he popularized two very important ideas: that psychology needs to be an objective science, and the need of society to use this science of behavior for social progress. These ideas would heavily influence future generations of behavioral psychologists, including the most important figure to date in the history of applied behavior analysis, B. F. Skinner.

As mentioned earlier, Skinner expanded upon Thorndike's work and refined trial-and-error learning into the system of operant conditioning, wherein behavior is seen in terms of its environmental consequences. The relationship between a behavior and its consequence is known as a "contingency." Put very simply, every behavior results in some stimulus being delivered to the organism. Stimuli that increase the probability of a behavior being emitted again are called "reinforcers." Stimuli that decrease the probability of a behavior being emitted again are called "punishers." Both reinforcers and punishers can be positive or negative. This is not a value judgement, however. *Positive* refers to when a stimulus is presented, and *negative* refers to when a stimulus is withdrawn. Stimuli are not reinforcers or punishers in and of themselves; they must be considered in terms of their behavioral effects. Reinforcers increase the future probability of a given behavior while punishers decrease the future probability of a given behavior. That is how consequential stimuli are defined, and not in terms of their desired effects:

1. If an employee is praised for calmly dealing with an irate client and the future probability of this behavior increases, that is positive reinforcement (in this contingency, remaining calm and handling a touchy situation professionally results in the presentation of a stimulus, the praise).

2. If an employee is nagged until an assignment is finished and the future probability of this behavior increases, that is negative reinforcement (in this contingency, finishing a task causes the withdrawal of a stimulus, the nagging).

3. If parents yell at their child for using their record albums as frisbees and the future probability of such behavior decreases, that is positive punishment (in this contingency, such destructive behavior produces a stimulus, yelling).

4. If, however, the child's bicycle is taken away for a week after the record throwing incident, and the future probability of such behavior decreases, that is negative punishment (in this contingency, destructive behavior causes the withdrawal of a stimulus, the bicycle).

Research into related topics, e.g., *schedules of consequences* (According to what system should the consequential stimuli be presented or withdrawn?), the process of *shaping* (creating new behavior by differentially reinforcing successive approximations to a desired behavior until the actual desired behavior itself is emitted), *stimulus control* (control by specific stimuli antecedent to the behavior), *rule-governed behavior* (how behavior is shaped by verbal descriptions of contingencies as opposed to the actual contingencies), *equivalence classes* (how stimuli become regarded as related), and *establishing operations* (What conditions contribute to the effectiveness of consequential stimuli?) continue to add to the power of this science. From the analysis of behavioral relationships, behavior analysts have constructed probably the most powerful system yet known for understanding as well as systematically and reliably altering behavior.

BEHAVIOR ANALYSIS AND
HUMANISM ARE COMPATIBLE

Like Watson before him, Skinner stresses behavior as the subject matter for psychology, and advocates applying the process and findings of behavior analysis to the problems faced by society. Also like Watson, Skinner has a remarkable ability to make people angry. A final commonality is that Skinner's thought is highly misunderstood:

1. It is said that Skinner denies the existence of thinking. He does not. Skinner does assert, however, that thinking (considered "covert" behavior) is subject to the same laws as more overt behavior (a belief held by many philosophers, including William James [1842–1910]). Thoughts are considered by Skinner as links in the full behavior chain. Thoughts may function as rehearsals for more overt behavior, or provide consequences for overt behavior. When this fact is appreciated, many of the objections against the behavioral system are negated. For example, it is often claimed that behaviorism, because it neglects "inner life," cannot do justice to the complexity of the human mind and how the mind affects our behavior. What the behavioral system actually provides is a parsimonious framework from which to view mental life and its behavioral effects.

There are times when the consequences maintaining a given behavior are not readily apparent. In order to avoid "invoking action at a distance" (suggesting that a temporally distant consequence is maintaining behavior), we must seek fairly immediate consequences. Take, for example, a woman who has learned through modeling (learning by observation) and reinforcement to perform the rituals of a particular religion. She is then transplanted into a totally secular environment, with no contact with others of her religion and therefore with no social consequences to maintain her behavior. She continues to perform her rituals. To explain this, we must look to "rule-governed" behavior (Malott 1986).

According to the theory of rule-governed behavior, through both the experience of particular contingencies and external verbal descriptions of contingencies (e.g., "Don't touch that or you'll get burned"; "Stop that or you'll go blind"), we acquire internal verbal descriptions of behavior-consequence relationships. When we follow a rule, we reinforce our behavior with congratulatory self-statements ("I am a good person for having done this"). When we break a rule, we punish our behavior through denigrating self-statements ("I am terrible for having broken this rule"), and guilt or anxiety may be generated by these cognitions. It has been theorized that much "self-managed" behavior is therefore maintained by negative reinforcement (anxiety or guilt is taken away by performing behavior in keeping with a particular rule [Malott 1986]).

As a further example of how radical behaviorism's conception of mental life can help us explain complex human behavior, consider the Freudian defense mechanisms. According to psychoanalysis, when unacceptable impulses or memories threaten to invade consciousness, defense mechanisms (e.g., sublimation or repression) are employed to help the ego deal with the anxiety. The underlying idea is somewhat hydraulic: an unacceptable impulse or memory is "pushed down" into the unconscious. It then attempts to "push" its way into consciousness, and must be "redirected" or "disguised" somehow.

Skinner (1974, pp. 170-174) has made the point that these types of "defenses," which it seems are fairly common, can be explained without employing the questionable theoretical baggage of the Freudian system. This can be done by simply considering defense mechanisms as examples of covert behavior and thinking of them in terms of behavioral consequences. As Skinner states (1974, p. 172), "we have 'repressed our rage' because we have been punishing for 'expressing it.' " When we again express our rage (covertly), we may engage in self-punishment in the form of anxiety or guilt. We are likely to seek ways (the defense mechanisms) to behave that will maximize reinforcement and minimize punishment (Skinner 1974, p. 173): "a person defends himself against punishment by acquiring behavior effective in the world in which he lives (as ego), reinforced in part because of susceptibilities to reinforcement which are part of his genetic endowment (as id), and not punished by other persons or by himself (as superego)."

2. It is said that Skinner neglects biology, relying solely on behavioral conditioning. This is not true. Biological evolution is recognized as the first determinant of behavior. It is also untrue that Skinner denies the value of physiological research. He does state, however, that the need will always exist for behavioral analyses in understanding behavior.

3. *It is said that Skinner's political system would be oppressive.* This is not true. Skinner recognizes that, most often, positive reinforcement is more powerful than punishment in altering behavior, and that punishment often yields unwanted side-effects (see chapter three). America's current legal system relies heavily upon punishment, while Skinner's system emphasizes positive reinforcement. This is a point that will become important: our judicial/legal system does attempt some use of behavioral control, but not in a way consistent with the findings of behavior analysis.

4. *It is said that Skinner could not, according to his own theory, create a new system of psychology.* This argument springs from a misconception regarding behavior analysis, that it only deals with the reinforcement of pre-existing behavior and cannot account for behavior not already emitted by the person. There are at least two reasons why this is inaccurate. First, there is the shaping process, where successive approximations to a desired behavior are reinforced until the target behavior is emitted and reinforced. The clinical literature is full of examples in which a behavior analyst differentially reinforced behavior that only vaguely resembled a portion of the target behavior until the full, complex behavior was emitted.

Second, there is the extinction process. When a behavior is no longer reinforced, an organism will reliably increase its level of activity and emit new responses, the "extinction burst." One of these new responses may be reinforced and maintained in the behavioral repertoire. Thus, if a given theory was no longer successful in accounting for observed phenomena, then a scientist's responding (i.e., following old paradigms) would undergo extinction and new theories would be synthesized.

5. *It is said that Skinner seeks to rob humanity of its dignity and to reduce people to robots.* This is also not true, and this is crucial to the point. It is true that Skinner, believing as he does that environmental and genetic forces shape the behavior of the

organism, believes that giving credit or assigning blame to an individual is a pointless exercise, except in that these are consequential stimuli that serve to shape behavior. Skinner does not seek to turn humanity into robots. He merely advocates the application of the principles of science to human behavior, which would seem to be a rather humanistic idea according to the definition and tradition of humanism (a conclusion supported by Skinner being honored as "Humanist of the Year" for 1972 by the American Humanist Association). To illustrate this point, I have set up the following chart. On the left side are statements about humanism, taken from Corliss Lamont (1982, pp. 12-14). On the right side are statements I have taken from Skinner's writings which correspond to the points made by Lamont.

Lamont	Skinner
1. "Humanism believes in a naturalistic metaphysics . . . (and) considers all forms of the supernatural as myth."	"A particular practice may be recommended because it maximizes some such entity as salvation or the glory of God. Such justifications are presumably beyond the realm of science" (Skinner 1953, p. 358).
2. "Humanism, drawing especially upon the laws and facts of science, believes that man is an evolutionary product of the Nature of which he is part. . . ."	"Behavior has also come within the scope of a scientific analysis. It is a product of . . . selection, the first of which, natural selection, is the field of ethology. The second, operant conditioning, is the field of behavior analysis" (Skinner 1989, p. 27).

3. "Humanism . . . believes that human beings possess the power or potentiality of solving their own problems, through reliance primarily upon reason and scientific method applied with courage and vision."

"Almost all our major problems involve human behavior. . . . What is needed is a technology of behavior, but we have been slow to develop the science from which such a technology might be drawn" (Skinner 1971a, p. 22).

4. "Humanism . . . believes that human beings, while conditioned by the past, possess genuine freedom of creative choice and action, and are, with certain objective limits, the masters of their own destiny."

"In the behavioristic view, man can now control his own destiny because he knows what must be done and how to do it" (Skinner 1974, p. 277).

5. "Humanism believes in an ethics or morality that grounds all human values in this-earthly experiences and relationships and that holds as its highest goal the this-worldly happiness, freedom, and progress . . . of all mankind."

"(in *Walden Two,* Skinner's literary utopia based upon applied behavior analysis) . . . People are truly happy, secure, productive, creative, and forward-looking" (Skinner 1986/1965, p. 364).

6. "Humanism believes that the individual attains the good life by harmoniously combining personal satisfaction and continuous self-development with significant work and other activities that contribute to the welfare of the community."

"Now, among the specifications which might reasonably be submitted to a behavioral technology are these: Let people be happy, informed, skillful, well-behaved, and productive" (Skinner 1982a, p. 137).

7. "Humanism believes in the widest possible development of art and the awareness of beauty."

"There is no reason why a behavioristic account could not list the reinforcing effects of works of art, music, and literature . . ." (Skinner 1974, p. 206).

8. "Humanism believes in a far-reaching social program that stands for the establishment throughout the world of democracy, peace, and a high standard of living. . . ."

"The fact is, I accept the ends of a democratic philosophy, but I disagree with the means which are at the moment most commonly employed. I see no virtue in accident. . . . I believe that we must plan our own future and that we must take every advantage of a science of behavior in solving the problems which will necessarily arise" (Skinner 1982b, p. 34).

9. "Humanism believes in the complete social implementation of reason and scientific method. . . ."

"Nothing short of a better understanding of human behavior will solve our problems, and I still believe that this means better science and technology" (Skinner 1989, p. 120).

10. "Humanism, in accordance with scientific method, believes in the unending questioning of basic assumptions and convictions, including its own. Humanism is not a new dogma, but is a developing philosophy and open to experimental testing, newly discovered facts, and more rigorous reasoning."

"Experiments do not always come out as one expects, but the facts must stand and the expectations fall. The subject matter, not the scientist, knows best. . . . statements are constantly submitted to check . . ." (Skinner 1953, p. 13).

As we look over the contrasting statements, we note that the disparities are not as great as the horrible reputation of Skinner would prepare one to expect. Both Lamont, the humanist, and Skinner, the behavior analyst, subscribe to a naturalistic metaphysics. In this they exemplify the lack of regard for unprovables, particularly those that often lead to human suffering or a lack of progress, that humanists and behavior analysts seem to share.

Both believe in the evolutionary origin of humanity, and in the fostering and appreciation of beauty. Both believe in the importance of this-worldly thought and that the best interests of humanity as a whole should be paramount in any ethical system. Both claim to base their thinking upon science and advocate the application of science to the problems faced by humanity.

These last two points are where we run into a problem. Despite the congruence of thought displayed above, a real difference in belief exists. For Skinner, the behavior of an individual is determined by genetic endowments and reinforcement history. Lamont, while acknowledging the influence of conditioning, maintains a belief in free will. On a philosophical level, this issue of free will versus determinism need not present an insurmountable roadblock to an integration of these two systems. Lamont (1982, p. 163) admits that his belief in free will is only a "powerful intuition," and one does wonder how, without the disallowed intervention of some supernatural force, humanity came to have free will when determinism is so easily accepted in other animals.

Perhaps this whole controversy can be avoided, however. If free will does indeed exist, then destructive interventions attempted by behaviorists will be ineffective and they will therefore be discredited. This will do more to destroy the influence of behaviorists than any philosophical treatise (as flippantly suggested by Papanek [1973] and very nicely amended by Nord [1974]). If the behavioral interventions are successful, however, then we had better take them seriously. Those with a less-than-democratic agenda will use them, even if those in favor of democracy do not. In this same vein, it is interesting to note that champions of free will do not dispute the effectiveness of behavioral interventions. Even supposed anti-behaviorist Aldous Huxley (1958, p. 139) mentioned *Walden Two* as a possible solution to the problems pushing society toward his *Brave New World,* and described (in glowing terms) a society that used "Pavlov for positive purposes" in his last novel, *Island.* In any case, this can probably be reduced to a non-issue. Both humanists and behavior analysts accept the covert behavior of the mind. Those who believe in free will can certainly accept the notion that behavior analysis works because the individual freely decides to behave in a particular fashion. The behavior analyst can believe in the determinism that has traditionally been accepted in the discipline. Working from this deterministic framework, behaviorists, for their part, have devoted much energy to studying "choice" (decision-making) over the past twenty years (e.g., Rachlin and Green 1972). They have successfully described many factors which shape the form of decisions.

When we move past the realm of philosophy and enter the real world of applications, however, the controversy between free will and determinism becomes more pronounced. Skinner's society would provide positive reinforcers to encourage constructive behavior (as in More's *Utopia*). This generally sends humanists, who consider behavioral conditioning outright manipulation (e.g., Bettelheim 1987), into an uproar. With their belief in the protection of perceived freedom, the humanists regard any efforts at social planning as virtually synonymous with fascism. Skinner responds in three ways. First, behavior analysts are under the control of contingencies; they are therefore just as much "manipulated" as "manipulator." Second, he points out that our current social system already uses behavioral contingencies, although not in a way consistent with the findings of behavior analysis (e.g., lack of reinforcers and an emphasis on aversives [see chapters 3 and 5]). Third, he maintains that behavior is manipulated anyway, manipulated by the environment, and thus it is better to structure this environment so that constructive behavior is more probable. Leaving it to chance often leads to contingencies favoring destructive behavior (Skinner 1989). At the outset I suggested that humanism and radical behaviorism are two of today's most anxiety-provoking systems of thought. The humanists elicit anxiety when they suggest that there is no supernatural order, leading to a fear of the breakdown of society. The behavior analysts provoke anxiety when they suggest that there is real order to behavior, leading to a fear of the regimentation of society.

The only way to resolve this dilemma is to lay down a gauntlet with regard to stated philosophy and stated intentions. Taking a hard look at the beliefs of both the humanist and the behavior analyst, I think we must decide in favor of the behavior analyst. The fact that behavior is determined is scientific fact. In literally thousands of experiments, behavior has been shown to change, change back, and then change back again in keeping with environmental contingencies. The humanist, while giving lip service to the natural status of humanity and bold applications of science to the problems of society, stops short when it comes time to actually implement strategies that have been derived from scientific analysis.

This is not to say that the humanists do not have reason to be cautious about such applications. Applied behavior analysis is a very powerful system. The potential danger of an abuse of this science is very real and important to keep in mind. Simply because something has the potential to be abused is no reason to deny its use when it can achieve great good, however. In the rest of this book I shall attempt to show that behavior analysis has been used to achieve extremely beneficial ends and that the potential for even greater applications exists. I will also show that attempts to apply traditional humanist ideas have often had less than encouraging results. This is not to say that the goals of humanism are not worthy goals; they are. What they lack is a method of implementation. Applied behavior analysis provides this method.

The real character and mission of the behavior analyst was summed up by Skinner (1971b, p. 35):

> The behaviorists I know . . . are gentle people, deeply concerned with the problems facing us in the world today, who see a chance to bring the methods of science to bear on these problems, and who are fully aware of the dangers of the misuse of the power they are creating . . . behaviorism *is* humanism. It has the distinction of being effective humanism.

Because of its emphasis on science and the this-worldly benefits to humanity (as well as other similarities discussed earlier), a case could be made that behaviorism is already an extension of humanism itself (and not merely a humanitarian enterprise). While this is probably true, such a conclusion ignores the reality of the usage of behaviorism. Behavior analysis is humanistic when applied for the ends described by Dr. Skinner. There is no reason why it must necessarily be used that way, however. At the outset I stated that both humanism and applied behavior analysis contain flaws, and require one another to correct these flaws. Applied behavior analysis is a science. It describes what is, and can predict what will be. As a science, it cannot answer questions of implementation other than in utilitarian terms, and thus behavior analysis requires humanism to guide applications and ensure that a Frankenstein's monster is not created. This is not yet another call to "humanize science." Rather, this is a suggestion that humanism is the philosophy most in keeping with our current level of knowledge and one that leads to maximum benefit for all humanity. Humanism makes no provisions for a way to implement its goals, however. Applied behavior analysis supplies this method. This is, therefore, a call for contingencies to be structured such that behavior compatible with the humanist philosophy becomes prevalent.

2

Applied Behavior Analysis, Humanism, and Psychotherapy

QUESTION: How many psychotherapists does it take to change a light bulb?

ANSWER: Only one, but the light bulb has to really want to change.

PARTY GOER #1: I had my tenth anniversary with my psychoanalyst today.

PARTY GOER #2: That's a long time. Are you getting better?

PARTY GOER #1: No, but I hate to think what I'd be like if I wasn't going!"

Should I write off my psychotherapy costs as a medical expense or as a religious contribution?

The first joke is a standard, the second is adapted from Kendler (1981), and the third is respectfully stolen from Woody Allen.

THE LEGAL STATUS OF PSYCHOTHERAPY

A caption that was written for an earlier writing on psychotherapy (Newman 1989) reads "Treatments that work, rather than theories that work, should be the aim of any truly humanistic psycho-therapy." This statement sums up what I believe should be (but often is not) the guiding ethic in psychotherapy: conduct the enterprise as a science, and do what you have to do in order to help the client get better. When conducting therapy as a science, therapists continually measure progress so as to avoid ineffective procedures and to build on the knowledge of what is effective. In this way, both therapists and the profession come to understand the therapeutic process. Currently, the process is poorly understood.

The article mentioned above began with the true story of a patient suffering from severe depression. He was admitted to a psychiatric institution, where his psychiatrist, dedicated to psycho-dynamics, decided to forego treating the depression, opting instead for a "more ambitious goal" of treating an underlying personality disorder. After several months, during which his condition de-teriorated, the patient transferred to another institution. There he received anti-depressive medication and supportive psychotherapy. He made rapid progress, was subsequently discharged, and filed a malpractice lawsuit against the first institution. The defendants claimed that the lawsuit proves that the patient's personality disorder remains untreated (Malcolm 1986).

What was truly fascinating when the essay was published was the dichotomy of reactions I received.* The reactions to the article were mixed and broke down neatly by population. With few exceptions, the psychologists who saw the article gave me a verbal pat on the head and said that as I learned more I would see the holes in my argument. The laypeople who saw the article opened their eyes wide as I described the situation in psychotherapy, and often followed up by telling me their own horror stories (as if suddenly aware that they were not the only people to have had

---

*Notwithstanding a crime victim I was counseling who, after seeing the picture published along with the essay, said, "You were so handsome." Were? My hair had gotten longer in the years since the picture was taken, but I hadn't had an industrial accident or anything.

bad experiences). Many were young adults who had been finan-
cially blackmailed into therapy by their parents for the felonious
and intolerable offenses of being homosexual or taking part in
leftist political activities. (It is no accident that the repertoire of
"rebellion rock" band The Ramones includes such titles as "Shock
Treatment," "Psychotherapy," and "Teenage Lobotomy," while still
others include such lines as "they want to put me in a sanitarium.")
One letter I received in response to the article read, in part, "I
am a bipolar who has suffered at the hands of many so-called
mental health givers. Their damage to me is permanent." I do
not mean to say that psychotherapy is useless, or to fall into the
fanaticism that psychotherapists are puppets of our fascist state.
What I do mean to say is that psychotherapists are given an almost
shaman-like status in our society, which is intolerable. They are
professionals providing a service, and must be judged accordingly.

The basic state of affairs in psychotherapy is one of lawlessness.
Methodologically limited only by imagination, anyone may call
(him)herself a psychotherapist and practice in any way (s)he sees
fit (Ehrenberg and Ehrenberg 1986). L. Ron Hubbard, although
a fair science fiction writer, had no formal training in behavioral
science. He nonetheless created the psychotherapy school of
"Dianetics," which later became the Church of Scientology. The
general public is not aware that his system consists of outdated
ideas about the mind and discarded Freudian notions (Gardner
1957), or that Scientology has taken on the status of a cult (Randi
1982). They do not know these things because such embarrassments
are not often mentioned, for fear of a public outcry for regulation.
This state of virtual anarchy is encouraged by professionals who
fear regulation and thus perpetuate the idea that there is something
mystical about psychotherapy, something that defies description.
Corsini (1984, pp. 1-2), editor of widely read texts on psychotherapy,
begins with a dictionary definition:

> (psychotherapy is) a process of interaction . . . for the purpose of
> amelioration of . . . areas of (psychological) malfunction . . . with
> the treatment party having some theory of personality's origins,
> development, change . . . and some treatment logically related to
> the theory.

This definition not being comprehensive enough, he then adds:

> There is no way to settle any differences, so even though A and B may be doing . . . different and contradictory things, both are doing psychotherapy. . . . What some authority considers . . . psychotherapy may differ from how another . . . sees the process.

There are a few hundred brands of psychotherapy on the market, most with little more than anecdotes to back up their claims of effectiveness. This has done nothing to lower psychotherapy's popularity, however, as satirized by Gross (1986, p. 315): ". . . more patients now scream, touch, feel, jump, play, strip, and tickle their way to emotional perfection." (The tickling that Gross refers to is probably Z Process Therapy, also known as Rage Reduction or Attachment Therapy, where clients were held motionless while being physically and verbally "stimulated." One client suffered kidney failure as a result of "therapy" [Meyer, Landis, and Hayes 1988].) The unfortunate fact is that most schools of therapy have never been proven effective. The majority opinion among psychotherapists, however, seems to mirror Corsini's view that treatment techniques are virtually equivalent (a fact denied by clinical research), and therefore treatment should be dictated by therapist preference (Giles 1990).

Without strict adherence to the scientific method, psychotherapists run the risk of following questionable case study evidence. Murray (1974), for example, was so impressed by the chance statement of an autistic individual (which probably was an example of echolalia, the repeating of previously heard words, a common characteristic of autism) that he was prepared to suggest a whole new course for the treatment of the disorder. Fortunately, the weakness in Murray's conclusions, as well as his lack of expertise in the subject matter, was pointed out by Schreibman and Lovaas (1974). Case studies are highly convincing, but notoriously unreliable. Examples of these difficulties can be seen in the work of Freud himself, whose famous Anna O., for example, was found to be taking morphine to ease the symptoms Freud supposedly cured (O'Leary and Wilson 1987, p. 361).

At its worst, this failure to appreciate the scientific method can lead to psychotherapy becoming nothing more than hypocritical abuse. Let us take the case of the Orthogenic School of Bruno Bettelheim. Dr. Bettelheim (1987) subscribed to a psychoanalytic theory of the etiology of autism,* postulating that parents were the cause of their child's disorder. He therefore attempted to treat the disorder (which evidence suggests is probably biological in origin) by raising children diagnosed with autism in an environment suggested by psychoanalytic theory. Despite an inability to demonstrate the efficacy of his program (while simultaneously describing demonstrably effective programs as similar to those he encountered during his own concentration camp experiences), for almost forty years Bettelheim refused to change his program to one with demonstrated efficacy (Torisky 1990). Perhaps out of frustration with his own lack of success, incidents of alleged brutality and degradation against the child patients have been reported (see *Washington Post,* August 26, 1990, and *Newsweek,* September 10, 1990). Torisky (1990, p. 12) compared Bettelheim to Rousseau in his hypocrisy, but then concluded:

> But this comparison is perhaps far too kind. Bettelheim would ultimately have to take personal responsibility for thousands of shattered lives before he left this earth. Unfortunately, his disciples still abound, spreading his flawed gospels throughout the world, and continuing to provide unthinking professionals with a framework for destructive family "therapy," and equally unthinking social agencies with excuses for inappropriate responses to the misery of autism.

Despite the fact that the effectiveness of most schools of psychotherapy has never been demonstrated, nothing prevents their continued use. Psychotherapy has become a popular and competitive field. In order for a school of psychotherapy to stand out, something new and different must be offered. This demand, coupled with a lack of regulation, has resulted in some of the wilder therapies on the market. This state of lawlessness is advocated by some, who believe that each therapist must do his/her own thing in order to be effective. A humanistic view of psychotherapy regards this

---

*A disorder marked by extreme social isolation, communication disabilities, and possibly excessive self-stimulatory or self-injurious behavior.

as an evasion of responsibility and an abuse of the client's right to effective treatment (e.g., Van Houten et al. 1988). The humanistic view of psychotherapy regards the physical and mental abuses that have occurred in the name of psychotherapy as morally reprehensible. Only slightly less offensive are those who practice parasitically; practicing as they see fit, regardless of how ineffective or ignorant of relevant research they may be.

THE HUMANISTIC VIEW OF PSYCHOTHERAPY

It's necessary to take a step back at this point. Commenting on the humanistic view of psychotherapy is a risky undertaking. Just as the meaning of the term "humanism" is open to philosophical debate, so, too, the term "humanistic" is a hotly contested adjective within psychotherapy. It has probably been applied to almost all of the 250-400 schools of psychotherapy by their individual proponents. One set of schools even identifies itself as "humanistic psychotherapy." To clarify this confusion, and to continue the task of demonstrating that applied behavior analysis and humanism are complementary systems, it is essential to trace the history of "humanistic psychotherapy." I hope this analysis will bring out three points: (a) that humanism, or any philosophy of life, is unavoidably value-laden and prescriptive, (b) what is humanistic is to help people, and (c) that psychotherapy can be put on a more solid scientific basis.

As mentioned earlier, the roots of humanistic philosophy can be traced back at least as far as ancient Greece. For the philosophical background of the humanistic psychotherapists, however, we should look at the Renaissance. Renaissance humanism, reacting against the religious excesses of medieval Christianity, was a philosophy of liberation that proclaimed the freedom and glory of humanity. History repeated itself in the 1950s and 1960s. Humanistic psychologists, reacting against the perceived excesses of psychoanalysis and behaviorism, proclaimed the birth of humanistic psychology, the "third force." By 1961, the *Journal of Humanistic Psychology* had begun publishing. Orthodox psychoanalysts had limited the study of humanity to unconscious conflicts, perceived by humanistic psychologists as bits and pieces of the total person. Behaviorism, with its reliance on determinism, dehumanized the individual. The study of the individual's behavior also limited the degree to which the whole person was the focus of research or therapy. The "third force," therefore, sought to return the total "self" as a valid focal point of research and therapy.

Although many powerful minds, including Karen Horney, Erich Fromm, Gordon Allport, Rollo May, and Kurt Goldstein, are identified with the movement, the two individuals who are most identified with humanistic psychology and psychotherapy are Carl Rogers and Abraham Maslow. Rogers was perhaps the more visible of the two. He did much to popularize the orientation, including taking part in well-publicized debates with B. F. Skinner (e.g., Rogers 1986 and Skinner 1986). His fame as the creator of Client-Centered (or Person-Centered) Psychotherapy also made him a natural spokesperson for the approach, a position he did not always relish (Rogers 1964). It was Maslow, however, who was the driving force behind the organization of the movement (Stagner 1988) and thus we will begin with his thought.

Although trained as an experimental psychologist, Maslow largely abandoned this discipline. As summarized by Kendler (1987, p. 423), "Maslow operated more like a humanistic philosopher who expansively theorized about human nature and human morality without any strong commitment to obtain supporting empirical evidence." Although not based on experimental evidence, Maslow's thought is nonetheless important, particularly in the areas of motivation and "human nature." Maslow's hierarchy, as his system for conceptualizing motivation is known, will prove essential to demonstrating the first point raised at the beginning of this section, that any world-view is essentially value-laden and prescriptive.

Maslow's (1970) hierarchy is a ladder-like system of needs that must be fulfilled on the way toward the "self-actualization" of the individual. The needs at the bottom of the ladder, which include those pertaining to physical survival, must be fulfilled before needs higher on the list (e.g., the need for social belonging) can be addressed. When people become self-actualized, they share a certain outlook, an outlook characterized by such things as a feeling of identification with humanity, a sense of realism, an acceptance of the self, benign humor, peak emotional experiences, and to some degree the desire and ability to reshape the social environment. By examining such individuals, Maslow thought he could discover the "correct" way to live.

In this desire to discover and suggest the proper way to live, Maslow is indistinguishable from Watson or Skinner. His views are embraced as humanistic, while those of Watson and Skinner are considered mechanistic and manipulative, largely because Maslow's system relies on factors inside the individual instead of external forces. Maslow's thinking is also not generally regarded as dangerous, because he did not offer concrete suggestions as to how to self-actualize. Nonetheless, he did present a picture of perceived perfect humanity and suggested that his system was a way to discover this perfection. Watson held to a different picture of perfect humanity. The latter preferred unemotional, strong, and efficient people to Maslow's self-actualized individuals. Surely, however, this is a matter of taste. Watson went further than Maslow in suggesting how his idea could be realized. Skinner went further still. Nonetheless, the underlying philosophy of all three is essentially the same.

This is in no sense a condemnation of Maslow. On the contrary, it is a compliment. A democracy requires the active participation of individuals from all points on the political spectrum. Maslow had the courage to suggest that his ideas were of serious importance and the genuine desire to see them applied for the benefit of humanity. He erred in failing to realize that his system was based on personal taste rather than objective criteria. I would argue, however, that at this point in history there has never been a completely value-free philosophy of life, and this includes the various manifestations of humanism. All are essentially value-laden and prescriptive in nature.

By their very nature, philosophies of life hold to certain conceptions of (i.e., contain certain assumptions about) humanity. Unlike sciences, which only describe what is and predict what will be, philosophies of life must inevitably hold views on what is good and bad for humanity, even if it amounts to extreme moral relativism. In this case, the value expressed is that it is wrong to interfere with someone else's individuality. To illustrate, consider one of the great characters from the annals of science fiction, "Avon," from the British television series "Blake's 7." A quote of Avon's, from an episode entitled "Children of Auron," is appropriate here: "Neutrality or pacifism, it all boils down to the same gutless inanity." Avon has brutally captured the point. Even the systems he berates, which seek to avoid influencing others, cannot help but do so. They are preaching values as strongly as anyone else. They believe they have found the proper way to behave, and act accordingly. To truly understand the nature of psychotherapy one must appreciate this point. With the exception of behavior analysis, all schools of therapy of which I am aware accept some view of humanity apart from the empirical data. They therefore accept a perceived concept of healthy humanity that dictates what the goals of therapy should be. Where the therapies differ of course is in their specific perception of healthy humanity (e.g., freeing people from unconscious conflicts, uncovering irrational thoughts, removing blocks to personal growth, etc.). To speak of systems being more or less prescriptive is nonsensical. The prescriptiveness of any given system does not derive from its methods, but rather from its perception of healthy humanity. Variations in systems usually occur in the validity of their respective assumptions and in the efficacy with which they carry out their objectives. Being a science that describes functional relationships between behavior and environmental stimuli and therefore having no established perception of healthy humanity, behavior analysts must "borrow" an outside philosophy to guide their interventions. There is nothing in behavior analysis itself that dictates what the goals of therapy should be; therefore, goals must be chosen on the basis of philosophical orientations outside of the system itself. Despite claims to the contrary, Maslow did not objectively discover the "healthy person." He merely took his own version of healthy humanity and reified it. He is not to be condemned for advocating his views, but by the same token we should not grant his views credence beyond that of being one man's personal vision.

Carl Rogers, in contrast to Maslow, made a conscious effort to avoid being prescriptive and attempted to maintain contacts with objective science. In my opinion he failed (albeit admirably) on both counts. As I have attempted to establish, no system of psychotherapy that separates itself from empirical data can avoid being prescriptive. And, because of the direction Rogers's system took, he lost contact with objective science.

Rogers is best known as the creator and proponent of Client-

Centered therapy, the core assumption of which is derived from one of Rogers's (1961, pp. 11-12) experiences as a psychotherapist:

> (Rogers realized that) it is the *client* who knows what hurts, what directions to go, what problems are crucial, what experiences have been deeply buried. It began to occur to me that unless I had a need to demonstrate my own cleverness and learning I would do better to rely upon the client for the direction of movement in the process.

As can be inferred from this belief, subjective experience is given a great deal of weight in Rogers's system (1961, p. 24): "Neither the Bible nor the prophets—neither Freud nor *research* (emphasis mine) . . . can take precedence over my own direct experience." Rogers's therapy is therefore carefully constructed to provide the proper environment for the client to lead the therapeutic process. A premium is put upon the way the therapist interacts with the client. Empathy, unconditional positive regard, and "being real" are some of the characteristics of a good Client-Centered therapist.

Clinical research early in the development of the therapy seemed to confirm Rogers's theories. In this attempt to objectively research psychotherapy, Rogers was something of a pioneer and is to be heartily congratulated. Unfortunately, he did not continue with this effort. Late in his career, he uncritically endorsed the encounter group movement and even expressed some "New Age" beliefs. Rogers's own Client-Centered system also changed little with further research. His guiding philosophy became the centerpiece of therapy, rather than the impetus for experimentally demonstrating efficacy.

Rogers took his philosophy very seriously. In debates with Skinner and in his own writings, Rogers stated in no uncertain terms that he wanted no part of a behaviorally designed society. His conception of the therapeutic process, which he considered prototypical of a growing experience on the way to "becoming a person," was (so he believed) the exact antithesis of the behavioral approach. The very freedom Rogers considered so central to human growth was supposedly crushed by the behavioral orientation.

Although Rogers attempted to avoid being prescriptive by allowing clients to lead the therapeutic process and in so doing to develop their own potentials, he set an impossible task for himself. His own view of humanity was that of the developing individual, and this hope is embodied in his system. Rogers's therapy could not help but encourage "development" (i.e., behavior change) in keeping with his preconceived ideas. This is a phenomenon common to all psychotherapies. Therapists reinforce behavior that coincides with their theoretical orientations (Goldstein and Krasner 1987). Clients, therefore, often emerge as "converts," seeing themselves and their (hopefully) former problems in light of the therapist's orientation.

What is it that characterizes the "humanistic psychotherapy" of the "third force"? First, there is a concern with the individual as a whole. Second, there is a belief that individual freedom of choice is crucial. Third, there is an emphasis on the development of the individual, and a structuring of the therapeutic process to aid in this development. Looking at the definition of humanism offered in chapter one (see page 14), is there anything necessarily humanistic about this orientation? I think not, at least no more so than most schools of psychotherapy could claim.

To return to the sentiment expressed in the beginning of this chapter, humanism uses the methods of science to alleviate human suffering. If it is the case that humanistic psychotherapy uses the scientific method to aid troubled individuals in relieving their difficulties, then that therapy can truly lay claim to being "humanistic." The therapies of the "third force" may indeed be the most appropriate and effective techniques for helping individuals who suffer from, for example, existential dilemmas (e.g., troubled college students) and who require a supportive environment to aid in "getting their heads straight." Note that it is the practice and results, not the philosophy, that designates these therapists as humanists. To cavalierly claim that a given psychotherapy is effective without substantiating this claim is hardly humanistic. The unfortunate truth is that many problems in living will not be alleviated by empathy, a supportive environment, or even unconditional positive regard.

PSYCHOTHERAPEUTIC RESEARCH

How can we know, it might be asked, what type of therapy will be effective? There are some general guidelines one can follow in answering this question. Congruence between clients' views of what therapy *should* be like and what the clients actually experience is correlated with positive results (Bruckner-Gordon, Gangi, and Wallman 1988). There is also a clinical literature of studies that attempts to establish the efficacy of various forms of therapy for specific disorders (e.g., Giles 1983, Paul 1966). Consulting this literature can give insight into the type of therapy required for a given problem; therapists should keep up with current research concerning problems they often see in practice.

The problem with the general guidelines suggested above is just that; they are general. Most research in psychotherapy is conducted in a between-groups research design. In this type of research, there are generally two or three different groups exposed to different conditions. Every effort should be made to render the subjects in each of these groups equivalent with regard to relevant factors, e.g., age, gender, type of problem, severity of problem, education level, etc. Equivalence is striven for by assigning individuals into groups randomly. These equivalent groups are then exposed to either a form of therapy that is being tested, some standard form of therapy that leads to predictable levels of success, or possibly a placebo or waiting list control group. By comparing the average levels of success for each group, it is believed that the most effective psychotherapy methods can be discovered. There is some merit to this approach. There are, however, serious problems as well.

Because between-groups research relies on the average results of a group, the observed results may not represent the actual results for any individual. Some people might have gotten better. Some might have gotten worse. Some might not have changed at all. With a between-groups design there is no way to know how therapy affected any specific individual. Also, in a between-groups design there is no way to know what it was about the therapy in question that led to the observed results, at least not without running an entirely new experiment. Measures of before and after success rates are not of much help in isolating the crucial component of therapy (i.e.: Was it the client-therapist relationship, specific exercises, client insight, or some other variable that led to improvement?). In keeping with the prophecies of critics of my essay mentioned at the beginning of this chapter, I have learned that my thinking was indeed incomplete. The idea that psychotherapists need to be treated more like professionals and less like shamans still holds. What was lacking (in addition to all references, cut by the editor) was an exploration of single-subject research.

Another type of research which may prove more efficient in evaluating psychotherapy is the single-subject design, the design used in applied behavior analysis. As the name suggests, single-subject research is conducted with only one individual as the subject. In this research, a "baseline" period of observation prior to therapeutic intervention is conducted in order to determine the level of a given problem. Some intervention is then implemented, the level of the problem still being monitored. If acceptable progress is not attained, another intervention is attempted until one that works satisfactorily is found. In some instances (the reversal design) the therapy may be terminated (a return to baseline) to see if the gains of therapy are maintained. If they are not, then a return to the intervention phase of research is conducted and it can safely be concluded that the variable controlling behavior has been identified. In other instances the therapeutic intervention (almost always assumed by the client or significant others in the client's environment, e.g., reinforcing assertiveness or providing consequences for depressive behavior) is continued for as long as necessary, and then gradually faded out as the natural environment begins to control the new, adaptive behavior. In another method of single-subject research, the "multiple baseline," the key question is whether or not the problem is alleviated across subjects whenever a particular intervention was instituted (whenever baseline was terminated) during the therapeutic process. The multiple baseline is generally more appropriate when the removal of a given intervention would not be expected to lead to behavioral deterioration. Once reading has been taught, for example, we would not expect a person to lose this skill because a teaching program has ended. (A detailed discussion of the various forms of single-subject research is beyond the scope of this volume. Readers are referred to Cooper, Heron, and Heward [1987] and to Kazdin [1982] for excellent discussions of the topic.)

Single-subject research has an advantage over between-groups designs in that the individual is always the focus of research, and thus any statements made about the results of therapy are specific to the individual (and not to some group average which may not be representative of anyone). Single-subject research also has an advantage in that it is possible to know exactly when and why therapeutic gains are made. With a number of individual single-subject experiments, it is possible to establish that each time a given intervention was implemented, it led to improvement across subjects or environments. Some (e.g., Baer 1989) have suggested that the choice of research strategy is simply a matter of taste. Others have been more particular, insisting that either between-groups or single-subject research is the proper method. Both types of research have a place, depending on the questions to be addressed.

THE APPLIED BEHAVIOR ANALYSIS
VIEW OF PSYCHOTHERAPY

Applied behavior analysis takes a different view of psychotherapy than that espoused by Corsini above. The applied behavior analyst looks at the presented problem as a behavior which can be eliminated by use of single-subject research and behavior analysis as described above, provided the problem is not of biological origin, which may mean that medication is required. That a disorder is biological in origin does not, however, mean that behavior analysis cannot help alleviate symptoms. The key assumption is that the presented problem can be conceptualized in terms of the Antecedent-Behavior-Consequence (ABC) paradigm. It is further assumed that if the problem behavior is not biological in origin, it is a result of environmental forces and the individual's responses (including covert thinking responses) to these forces; therefore, the key to changing the behavior is to change the contingencies of the behavior (including "self-defeating" contingencies). For example, an individual may have had adopting a helpless, "sick," or depressed role reinforced by significant others in the environment. (S)he may even have internalized statements regarding how others must help because (s)he is too depressed to function. To alter this depressed behavior would require reinforcing more adaptive behavior, and also perhaps putting the cognitions regarding help-lessness on extinction and reinforcing more adaptive cognitions.

Behavior analysts have traditionally worked in environments where they could achieve a large degree of control over the consequences of an individual's behavior, e.g., the schools, institutions, and the workplace. One effort to bring behavior analysis into the adult psychotherapy situation is Functional Analytic Psychotherapy or FAP (Kohlenberg and Tsai 1987). "FAP leads the therapist into a caring, genuine, sensitive, involving, and emotional relationship with his or her client, while at the same time capitalizing on the clarity, logic, and precise definitions of radical behaviorism" (Kohlenberg and Tsai, p. 389). In FAP, an environment is created in which the client will demonstrate Clinically Relevant Behavior (CRB) during the therapy hour. In this way, the client can experience the contingencies of the actual problem behavior, rather than merely discussing them. Problems and goals are stated in explicit terms, in keeping with the practice of applied behavior analysis. Efforts are made to shape problem behavior into more adaptive behavior. While research into this procedure is still in the early stages, to the extent that practitioners of FAP maintain their practice in accordance with established applied behavior analysis (i.e., explicitly describing and being able to recognize target behavior when it occurs, establishing what conditions lead to the emission of target behavior, describing functional relationships between behavior and consequences, identifying reinforcers, promptly reinforcing improvements in target behavior, and making sure that behavior generalizes into the "real world"), they are building from a very solid base.

WHAT ARE ACCEPTABLE GOALS
AND STANDARDS FOR THERAPY?

In my work as a crime victim counselor, I was once approached by a woman who wanted me to help her adjust to the fact that her husband beat her. Understand, please, that this woman had three children, no marketable skills, did not want to leave her home and be cut off from a family who regarded her as a hysteric, could therefore not leave her husband, and was uncomfortable with going to a support group for battered women. While I felt tremendous conflict about it, I felt I could not work with her on this goal (getting used to being beaten). I offered to work with her on other, mutually agreeable goals. I could not believe that helping her to stay in the abusive relationship would be constructive. She declined the offer and sought help elsewhere.

Despite the extreme nature of this example, this was not an easy choice to make. My firm belief that no one should have to live in an abusive situation was balanced against my equally firm belief that no therapist should cavalierly set aside the goals of the client, or set goals that run contrary to the goals of the client. Could a person be helped to learn to accept beatings with minimal concern? I'm not sure, although I wouldn't be surprised, except at the lack of conscience on the part of the "helper." Again, we return to the idea that a technology exists to change behavior, but this technology in and of itself does not contain within it the ability to address whether a given behavior *should* be changed. Behavior analysts have created a series of ethical guidelines to address this problem. I think that these guidelines allow us to create what we should call "humanistic" therapy. (It should be noted that there is nothing proposed here that has not already been suggested by many others. Implementing the guidelines seems to be the tricky part.)

First, the client should be given all information needed in order to provide informed consent. This means the client is given an accurate description of what therapy will entail, what factors will determine length of therapy, the evidence for the efficacy of the proposed techniques, and any possible drawbacks or side-effects. Second, the goal of therapy should be, in the phrasing of behavior analysts, to maximize long-term reinforcement for the client. In common language, the goal of therapy should be to help the client *get* better, not just *feel* better. In the case of the woman described above, helping her to feel better about being beaten would have been a clear violation of this standard. The long-term functioning of the client should be considered and not just some short-term goal, except to the extent that the short-term goal will lead to maximum benefit in the long-term.

Third, less aversive techniques should be used in preference to more aversive techniques. This includes not only the actual therapeutic techniques, but also such things as frequency of therapy and cost. However, when less aversive techniques have been exhausted and have been documented as ineffective, then more aversive techniques may be used after consultation with the proper ethics board. This is a controversial point and will be discussed in the next chapter.

Fourth and finally, we return once again to our theme. Therapy should be conducted in accordance with our best available scientific evidence regarding what is most effective. While taking the clinical literature into account, therapists should consider each individual case as another experiment and proceed, always monitoring progress and never assuming that this case will necessarily be like any other encountered before.

When I was researching available academic programs in graduate psychology, I noticed that most graduate programs in clinical psychology subscribe to something they call the "scientist-practitioner" model. According to this model, therapists regard themselves as scientists and conduct therapy very much in accordance with what has been discussed here. Many of my graduate school classmates were at one time enrolled in such programs. They then left these programs in disgust at their professors' failure to live up to the stated philosophy. Instead of science, they were taught a "guru" approach to therapy. When all is said and done, it's time to leave the shamanism behind.

3

Can/Should We Teach Morality?

When I decided to include a chapter on morality in this volume, I knew I was treading on dangerous ground. Besides the fact that discussions of morals are usually vague discussions of ideology, behavior analysts are not particularly welcome in this area (Kohlberg 1983, p. x):

> Though valid for explaining many research findings,.Skinner's theory is not a valid educational theory in the sense of being a basis for good educational practices, a good theory for teachers to learn and follow. Skinner may dispense with ideas of freedom and dignity to arrive at a theory valid for explaining studies of reward in animals and children. A theory "beyond freedom and dignity" must, however, have serious flaws as a guide to teacher behavior. A theory that ignores freedom and dignity in the learning process leads to the practice of constructing "teacher-proof" materials. It also leads to kits designed to be "student-proof," that is, to modify the student's behavior without his understanding or assent to the theory and methods applied to him.

The first thing we should realize is that Kohlberg never really understood Skinner. Skinner did not say that "freedom and dignity" were real entities to be eliminated. Rather, he said that attributing behavior to some autonomous "inner being," separate and apart from the consequences of behavior, was an inadequate (and occasionally dangerous) strategy. Kohlberg's idea that behavior analysis is a theory primarily for animals and children is, although popular, anachronistic.

Kohlberg is concerned that Skinner and his behavioristic ilk commit what Kohlberg calls "the naturalistic fallacy," i.e., making the jump from "is" to "ought." As stated by Kohlberg (1983, p. xi), "Skinner makes this fallacy . . . in calling the good for children 'reinforcement.' " Returning to our definition of reinforcement from chapter one, it is again obvious that Kohlberg did not understand Skinner. And, as I have been attempting to demonstrate, behavior analysts do not commit the naturalistic fallacy. They do, indeed, state what is: behavior is influenced by its consequences. For their ought, however, they must reach outside their discipline. (Ironically, the charge has been made [e.g., Brinckerhoff 1971] that third-force humanists often commit the naturalistic fallacy in reverse; they believe that humanity *ought* to be a certain way, and then assume that humanity *is* that way. Like Horney's [1950] neurotics, third-force humanists create an idealized picture of humanity as a defense against life's harsh realities. Anything perceived as threatening this picture of the way things *should* be is anxiety-provoking, and defense mechanisms—e.g., denial, displacement, or rationalization—are mobilized to deal with the anxiety.)

The topic of a humanist leadership seminar I once attended was "moral education." Midway through the opening discussion, someone made the point that much "immoral" behavior is rewarded (e.g., students who cheat on exams often wind up with higher grades than they would have otherwise received). Following this observation, I raised the point that since immoral behavior is created and maintained by its consequences, then perhaps conversely the key to teaching morality is to arrange positive reinforcement for "moral" behavior. (Remember Skinner's quote from chapter one about there being no virtue in accident.) I mentioned that perhaps considering the problem from a behavioral perspective would lead to clearer answers and a plan of action.

From the reaction I received, one would have thought that I had suggested will-sapping brain implants. A chorus of "who has the right to do such a thing" murmurs went up before we moved on to the next point (rather quickly). In informal explorations of the issue later, one participant told me that behavioral consequences do not occur in nature. After we pursued the point and finally agreed that every behavior has a consequence, she said that she meant only to point out that human-based contingencies are artificial and therefore undesirable. (This issue will be explored later in this chapter). In keeping with our seminar readings of Kohlberg, most of the participants had no problem with accepting universal stages of moral development, apart from behavioral consequences. I stated that this was a remarkable claim, to which I received the reply, "Yes, it is a remarkable claim." Nonetheless, the claim was accepted. A subsequent lecturer specifically objected to the behavioral approach, claiming that its principles had been derived from animal research (the previously mentioned anachronistic argument) and animals, unlike humans, "cannot be inspired." Maybe, maybe not. That seemed like species chauvinism to me, and Wolfgang Kohler's (1887–1967) apes would probably disagree. Finally, behaviorism, so I was told, treats people as objects. This activity was then reified to "the root of all evil."

The problem seemed to center around the issues of control and deceit; the fear of "covert manipulation" was high. Later, we formally explored the issue. As one of our exercises, we broke up into small teams to tackle some issue of morality. In keeping with Kohlberg's "dilemma" approach to morality, my partners and I decided to examine the problem of farmers in the midwest. The farmers there are faced with a real moral dilemma—their farming chemicals are poisoning their groundwater. If they continue to use the chemicals, their groundwater will continue to be poisoned and eventually the entire area will face ruin. On the other hand, if they do not use the chemicals, they will be unable to grow their crops (so they believe, according to a midwestern participant), and their families will face ruin.

My two partners in this exercise, taking their lead from Paulo Freire (b. 1921), proposed that our plan of action should be to engage the farmers in a Socratic dialogue meant to "raise the farmers' consciousness." Through this dialogue, the farmers would eventually come to see the problems inherent in using the chemicals and would move toward more environmentally safe behavior. I proposed a more behavioral orientation to the problem, conceptualizing the issue not only as a problem with the behavior of the farmers, but also of the rest of the people involved in the farming effort. I outlined some behavioral interventions aimed at all parties involved. One of my colleagues refused to include this in our proposal, stating that behavioral interventions destroy people's humanity. In keeping with the previously expressed sentiment, the arguments against behavioral interventions rested on the fact that they (a) are manipulative and (b) destroy the humanity of the individual by treating them as objects. (Note that there was no discussion of effectiveness.)

We decided to make our presentations to the rest of the group separately. My two partners suggested their dialogue approach and stated why they felt my approach was unacceptable. In my own presentation I laid out my plan outlining how the intervention might proceed and then addressed the objections of my colleagues. They called the behavioral approach manipulative and suggested that the dialogue approach was not. I responded by saying that entering into a dialogue when you already know what the answer must be (a rigged game) was as manipulative as you could get, and that proposing to "raise peoples' consciousness" was not only treating them as objects, but a little arrogant as well.

The argument was surprisingly well-received. Even if the participants did not accept the behavioral approach, they at least acknowledged that we were all playing the same game, despite protestations of "noninfluence" (see chapter two). The general conclusion was that as long as interventions are aboveboard, as long as they are not "covert manipulation," then behavioral approaches are acceptable. We must act "with" and not "on." I suggested that the participants glance through the behavioral journals. They would then find that (a) their conceptions of behavioral research (e.g., studies done only with rats) were outdated, (b) their fears of behaviorists bent on covert manipulation were baseless, and (c) an effective behavioral technology, wisely applied, could go a long way toward solving many such problems. I also suggested that perhaps others with a less humanistic agenda would have no problem in attempting "covert manipulation," and that simply ignoring behavioral technology would not be helpful. We all finally agreed that our democracy relies on the active participation of all concerned and that we would do well to do whatever we could to see that the ends of "justice and kindness" (what we ultimately decided was an approximation of morality) are served.

Note that the solutions we proposed derived from the philosophical framework of humanism; in this case, that the good of all people, and not just oneself or one's family, should be considered in deciding a course of action. As has been repeated, behavior analysis sets no agenda in and of itself. It achieves goals set through some other mechanism. James Holland (1978), for example, who is a behavior analyst, has charged that behavior analysts too often serve the goals of the existing power structure in the United States (e.g., big business). He has gone so far as to describe the contingencies that direct the actions of behavior analysts in this regard. His charges deserve consideration and provide corroboration that the framework from which behavior analysts choose goals may need more attention.

It is difficult to arrive at an acceptable definition of morality that is not so vague as to be useless, and I'm personally not brave enough to attempt it. I'm also a little nervous about attempts to influence the "morality" of others (e.g., the efforts of the religious right to destroy the separation of Church and State and legislate conduct in accordance with their ideology). There are some areas of conduct, however, where I think we can all agree what the moral course of action is. I will now briefly discuss some prototypical work that behavior analysts have done in these areas. I think we would all agree that these efforts represent humanistic actions.

RACIAL INTEGRATION

There are few among us who would not accept as morally correct that people should be judged on criteria other than the color of their skin. Despite this widespread agreement, the problems of racism and other forms of prejudice are still with us and often flare up to dangerous proportions. Listening to the politicians, newspaper columnists, civic leaders, and talk-show hosts, it would be supposed that racism must first be attacked by altering attitudes. This strategy seems reasonable and simple enough. We harbor bad attitudes toward those of other races and must change these attitudes before constructive behavior will develop.

While this strategy may have some merit, there may be a still more effective approach available that we have been over-looking. The ultimate goal of these "attitude adjustments" is not really the changing of attitudes; it is the changing of our behavior toward one another. Perhaps, then, we should proceed in this direction: we should first alter the behavior, and expect that once favorable interactions begin, then favorable attitude change based upon these good experiences will follow. One pilot study that attempted to address this issue was conducted by Hauserman, Walen, and Behling (1973) almost twenty years ago.

In keeping with the suggestions of today's leaders, the anti-racism effort was conducted in the schools, with a small class of children. During baseline, the period of observation, it was noted that black children in the class isolated themselves (or, more probably, were isolated from the others involuntarily) during all nonstructured activities of a social nature. This occurred despite the teacher's verbal promptings for the children to make new friends (i.e., integrate and not isolate anyone). During the intervention phase of the study, the children received reinforcers for sitting with "a new friend" at lunch. (The color of the new friend was not specified.) During this phase of the study, black and white children sat together on over half of the opportunities. This "inte-gration" generalized into the nonreinforced after-lunch free-play period. Unfortunately, the study was of rather short duration, and the results were not as long-lasting as would be hoped once reinforcement was withdrawn. Despite this shortcoming, the study is significant in that it demonstrates that positive behavior changes with regard to racism can be addressed directly, and such direct intervention should be a part of any anti-racism effort.

RETURNING LOST ITEMS

To what extent does the motto "finders keepers" hold? We might be tempted to say that it depends on the person(s) who do the finding. If we know their "character" or "sense of morality," so the theory goes, then we can predict whether the item will be kept or an effort will be made to return it. Rather than discussing the character of the finder, however, perhaps we should consider the contingencies of the different options available to this individual. This line of thought was pursued by Goldstein, Minkin, Minkin, and Baer (1978).

Goldstein and colleagues noticed that in three local newspapers the number of lost ads consistently outnumbered the ads for items found. We might interpret this as a problem within the individuals who are doing the finding. They have found something and now they consider it theirs. We might even identify this as a lack of morality. Perhaps, however, the contingencies of the situation are such that seeking to find the real owner of a piece of property is not probable. This, indeed, turned out to be the case.

Placing a "found" ad in the newspaper is a financial burden for the individual who found the item. Perhaps it is asking too much of someone who has found property to pay money in the attempt to return it to its rightful owner. Fair enough. Across the three newspapers, when the fee for placing a "found" ad was removed, the number of such ads consistently outnumbered the number of "lost" ads, and the number of people who had their property returned increased. Before we look inside the person for moral behavior, we should look at the contingencies that govern the behavior.

SELF-HELP SKILLS

How often have we heard, and perhaps even thought ourselves, that those who are dependent upon public assistance are shiftless or unmotivated, somehow lacking in some other bit of "moral fiber"? In keeping with the previous example, perhaps we would do well to seek to explain their behavior in some way other than an appeal to moral weakness.

As will be discussed in greater detail in chapter five, the contingencies of the public assistance system are such that self-help behavior is not encouraged. If we are serious in expecting to help people on public assistance become more independent, we will have to stop punishing and start reinforcing self-help behavior. At least the first step in this effort was outlined by Miller and Miller (1970). As with the work on racist behavior discussed above, this research has been with us for about twenty years. (As will become especially apparent in chapter four, the findings of behavioral research are notoriously slow in making their way into public policy. I have purposely chosen examples of research that have been in the literature for many years because I wish to demonstrate that it is not a problem of the unavailability of such research, but rather of the findings not being implemented, perhaps due to prejudices [often based on misconceptions] against behavioral interventions.)

What the Millers did was quite simple. They reinforced attendance at self-help group meetings for public assistance recipients. Attendance at such meetings then increased by about 500 percent above baseline (i.e., prior to any reinforcement procedure being implemented). There was also some evidence that this behavior became generalized; attendees began to emit other self-help behavior (e.g., attending civic meetings, obtaining tutoring for their children, and the like). The purpose of the study was not to measure this generalization, so data on this was not systematically gathered. However, it does stand to reason that once individuals begin to receive reinforcement for self-help behavior, this behavior would be more probable than it would be in the absence of such reinforcement (or when it is punished, as is currently the case).

CRIMINAL IMMORALITY

What of those whose morality is at such a low level that they must be separated from society for our protection and for their (supposed) rehabilitation? Is criminal behavior under the rule of contingencies, or is there some defect in the moral character of these "moral imbeciles" (the old term for our current "anti-social personality disorder" diagnosis)? In yet another piece of research that is two decades old, Cohen and Filipczak's *A New Learning Environment* (1989/1971), that very issue was addressed.

In *A New Learning Environment* incarcerated teenagers were placed into a twenty-four-hour-a-day environment that reinforced pro-social and adaptive behavior. An emphasis was placed upon academic skills, an area where many criminal offenders are lacking. Inmates were given the option of living under standard institutional conditions or engaging in academic tasks for which they would be "paid," much like a regular job on the outside. The earnings from this learning could then be exchanged for special privileges or material items. When they began their project, Cohen and Filipczak (p. 6) were told that "this population consists of 'con men and freeloaders' and that, given the choice of free lodging, and food or earning better quality food, lodging, and clothing, they would choose to go on relief. This was simply not so."

What the researchers found was that young men, aged fourteen through eighteen, incarcerated for offenses ranging from car theft to homicide, would respond to this system. "We developed a system of extrinsic reinforcements which were already strong in the students' repertoires and which lent themselves to being altered gradually into the generally more desirable form of intrinsic reinforcement" (pp. 8-9). They also found that "anti-social" behavior was altered even in these "anti-social" individuals. In discussing the problem of inmate racism that threatened to flare up into violence, the researchers discuss the implications of their structured environment and the inmates: "The students were 'mixing it up.' They learned what most people learn—the loss of fear through familiarization. They also learned that one can have different friends for different reasons . . . (it was found that) such a system does work when it remains honest and consistent. It succeeds when it fulfills its commitment and delivers the choices and payoffs it promises" (pp. 84-85).

The follow-up news is both good and bad. The good news is that students posted impressive gains in terms of IQ scores as well as academic and work skills. Many were actually ready to rejoin society, a far cry from the "rehabilitation" currently received. At one year follow-up, the recidivism rate among graduates of the program was less than one-third that of a comparable standard program. Unfortunately, however, by the third year the recidivism rate for graduates of the program was near the norm for that of standard incarceration. How should we interpret this discouraging finding? There are at least three options: (a) the students were morally bankrupt and the program merely suppressed it for a while, (b) the students were conning the researchers and "playing the game," or (c) the "real world" environment outside the program failed to maintain the gains of the students.

In keeping with what we have discussed so far, I think we should choose option "c" as the most reasonable one. There was nothing wrong with the morality of the students. They were capable of pro-social and adaptive behavior, as evidenced by their conduct during the program. And, if students were just "conning" the researchers, then there would be no immediate difference in the recidivism between those in the program (but now out) and those from standard programs. The inescapable conclusion is that the outside world failed to live up to its responsibilities. Once released, the contingencies of the environment that had originally created and maintained the criminal behavior once again began to work. The sad fact is that the pro-social and academic behavior that was reinforced on the inside was not reinforced on the outside:

> The completed work . . . clearly demonstrates that not the young-ster but the public school system and its ecology have failed. The youngster is not mentally bankrupt but the public school and the systems that sustain it are. (Cohen and Filipczak 1989/1971, p. 5)

THE MORALITY OF BEHAVIOR ANALYSIS

I deliberately placed the discussion of inmates in a prison setting last, for reasons which will become apparent in a moment. I want to bridge from a discussion of the work done by behavior analysts in the area of morality to the question of the morality of behavior analysis itself. How can we attempt to use behavior analysis to encourage moral behavior when the very morality of behavior analysis itself has often been called into question? The most sensa-tional and well-known argument against behavioral interventions was raised by Anthony Burgess (and immortalized in film by Stanley Kubrick) in his novel *A Clockwork Orange*. The behavioral in-tervention received by Alex, Burgess's protagonist of sorts, was implemented in the prison setting.

For those not familiar with the story, *A Clockwork Orange* focuses on Alex, a teenager with a bad habit of committing "ultra-violence." Alex and his comrades commit random brutal robberies and violence, until Alex is finally turned upon by his friends and sent to prison. In prison, Alex volunteers for an experimental program that will allow him to leave the prison system within two weeks. In this experimental program, he is classically conditioned (via the pairing of an injected illness-inducing solution with movies of violence) to become violently ill when witnessing, or even thinking about, violence. The conditioning is successful, and Alex is released. On the outside, however, he is nearly helpless because of his conditioning. Alex's condition is exploited by political revolutionaries, who seek to use him as a symbol of the government's oppression (attempting to rig his suicide in the process). The government, realizing the danger Alex could pose, decondition him and promise to set him up with a good job in exchange for his support. The novel, and movie, ends with Alex realizing "I was cured all right," and planning to resume his life of ultraviolence. (In a twenty-first chapter not published in the United States until 1986, Alex freely decides that he is wasting his life and resolves to live more responsibly.)

The first question we should ask regarding *A Clockwork Orange* is "would such a conditioning procedure work?" Probably not. Perhaps in a controlled environment such as Alex's prison, where scenes of violence would only be paired with illness, the conditioning might last. On the outside, however, his getting ill would drop out via one of two routes. In the first scenario, once Alex was on the outside, he would inevitably be exposed to scenes of violence that were too minor to be illness-inducing (e.g., a play argument). Gradually, via a process similar to a clinical procedure known as systematic desensitization, Alex would be able to experience greater and greater scenes of violence without illness and would eventually partake of violence himself once again. The second route, known as flooding, would be the more probable end of Alex's conditioning. Here, phobic patients are exposed to an overabundance of that which makes them anxious. Although extremely uncomfortable, the clients learn that the phobic stimulus is not truly to be feared, and the anxiety decreases. In a society as fraught with violence as our own, Alex's anxiety would have flooded out rapidly. (In the book it is not clear how the government actually deconditions Alex. Alex has dreams, e.g., a dream of dirty water in his body being replaced with clean water, but that's as detailed as it gets. We are left to draw the conclusion that, while Alex was recovering from an attempted suicide and lying unconscious in a hospital bed, somehow the conditioning process was reversed.)

Whether or not Burgess's novel is consistent with what we know about behavioral interventions is not the real issue. Burgess was not trying to present a scientifically accurate case study. He was trying to make a point about the morality of behavioral interventions (and perhaps even more so about the morality of government intervention in our lives). As can be seen from the introduction to the 1986 version of the book, Burgess is rather upset with government's influence in our lives (and with "restrictive legislation"). His title, *A Clockwork Orange,* refers to "the application of a mechanistic morality to a living organism oozing with juice and sweetness" (Burgess 1986, p. xi). He insists that humans, by definition, have free will (p. ix). The only real answer to Burgess is to point to studies similar to those discussed above and to suggest that perhaps looking inside the person for free will isn't the answer. Burgess says that he's sick of discussing the issue. I'll respect his wish and move on. (But see Newman [1991] for a more detailed discussion of Burgess and his work.)

Behavioral interventions have been questioned on grounds besides the free will issue. First, behavioral interventions have been conceptualized as mere bribery, and it has been suggested that "unnatural" contingencies do not lead to the behavior being performed for its own sake. Second, it has been suggested that behavioral interventions only work under conditions of deprivation. Third, it has been charged that there is an overemphasis on the use of aversive stimuli. Fourth and finally, it has been suggested that the approach should be barred on ethical grounds separate and apart from any other considerations. This objection springs from the "behavioral interventions treat people like objects" argument. Each point will be addressed in turn.

First, there is the argument that behavioral interventions represent mere bribery and that the artificial and unnatural "extrinsic reinforcement" will lead to the behavior not being done for its own sake ("intrinsic reinforcement"). If this is indeed the case, then our entire social system consists of bribery and we are all living under unnatural extrinsic reinforcement. What's so natural about money, our most powerful and pervasive reinforcer? Our entire social system consists of contrived behavioral consequences (both reinforcers and punishers) that are delivered contingently upon certain types of behavior defined by the society as good or bad. Perhaps it is not as systematic as the behavior analyst would have it, but the difference is one of degree and there is still no virtue in accident. The issue of whether extrinsic reinforcement leads to the activity not being performed for its own sake was analyzed by Dickinson (1989) who found that the effect was weak and transient, and concluded that the whole debate regarding the detrimental effects of extrinsic reinforcement was "much ado about nothing" (p. 13).

An argument that springs from an anachronistic view of behavioral research states that behavioral interventions only work under conditions of deprivation. This reasoning is theoretically correct, but the argument misses a crucial point. It is true that an organism that has just finished a five course meal will not perform a task for a food reinforcer. Reinforcers used in most behavioral interventions are not so one dimensional, however. It is standard practice to use generalized reinforcers, those (e.g., money) that can be used for a great many commodities or privileges, or to have a wide "menu" of reinforcers that can be chosen. Using any sort of deprivation that would leave a subject without basic sustenance and activity is rarely called for, and can comfortably be reserved for those rare situations where lives are at stake (e.g., individuals with anorexia nervosa who must eat or they will die).

The third argument against behavioral interventions—that there is an overemphasis on aversive (punishing) consequences—has recently become a hot political topic. It is a basic tenet of the popular "Least Restrictive Model" that aversive consequences are used only as a last resort when nothing else has worked. There are many individuals, however, both inside and outside the profession, who feel that aversive consequences are used too often, or should not be used at all. Malott (1990) feels that this idea may have been taken too far, perhaps to the detriment of clients. He has made the point that behavior analysts and the last of the flower children are the only groups left in the world who believe that aversives can be eliminated. In contrast, Sidman is a behaviorist who feels that aversives are used too freely. In *Coercion and Its*

Fallout (1989) he outlines reasons why techniques based on aversives are unacceptable: punishment may lead to avoidance or escape efforts, and also to counteraggression. The behavior of the punisher may also be negatively reinforced, leading to escalations in the severity of punishment. Finally, while punishment may eliminate a given behavior, it does not teach any new, adaptive behavior; in fact, it may teach the punished to punish. While Sidman does admit that the need to use punishment procedures may exist, at least in emergencies, he does this only half-heartedly (p. 7):

> Many therapists are willing to accept restrictions on the use of coercive therapy, agreeing, for example, that they will not use coercion except when no positive procedure will solve the problem. In principle, I cannot dispute that well-meant and sensible condition. In fact, I believe the prerequisite—nothing else works—is rarely met. I would go so far as to say to anyone who claims to have tried everything else: "Tell me everything you did. I will then suggest a procedure you did not try." Undoubtedly, I would sometimes be unable to do this, but not, I believe, very often.

Ethical safeguards have been instituted to attempt to address this matter. In addition to the condition that all nonaversive techniques must be attempted and documented as ineffective before attempting an aversive procedure: (a) permission is requested from an ethics board with a report detailing previous efforts; (b) informed consent is provided by the client, a client's guardian, or a competent client advocate; (c) the aim of the intervention is to maximize long-range benefits for the client, and (d) constructive behavior is reinforced at the same time that destructive behavior is reduced. The client is not left "behaviorless."

Sidman's example of a cattle-prod-wielding therapist (p. 174) is thus something of an oxymoron and is certainly not consistent with the ethical use of behavior analysis (or its practical use, in view of the side-effects of punishers). Still, the debate continues. As a professor of mine once put it, it's very difficult to say that you're for punishment. It just doesn't sound right, like being pro-abortion (hence the more pleasing "pro-choice"). Who wouldn't want to be against the use of aversive procedures? Unfortunately, this isn't a matter of taking the moral high or low ground. Punishment is a natural and necessary phenomenon; its evolutionary function was to keep us from repeatedly engaging in dangerous behavior. It is no less necessary in modern life. In certain cases, punishment procedures prove to be the most effective techniques for eliminating potentially life-threatening behavior (e.g., self-mutilation).

Nonetheless, laws are pending in many states that would totally ban the use of aversives. While behavior analysts should welcome scrutiny of their procedures, it is highly questionable to ban procedures that alleviate suffering because they offend our sensibilities (Miron 1986). Even Sidman acknowledges that it may be unavoidable in certain instances to use "coercion," and also defends those who use aversive stimuli in an attempt to research this vital phenomenon (p. 12). I don't think many people enjoy inflicting suffering on others. However, by virtually eliminating the use of some aversive procedures, policy makers are inflicting even more pain by allowing some potentially life-threatening behavior to go untreated by the most effective means possible.

Fourth and finally, it has been suggested that behavioral interventions, because they supposedly treat individuals like objects, are to be barred on purely moral grounds. To respond to this argument, I will rely on two individuals discussed at the humanist conference on moral education referred to earlier. The first of these individuals was John Rawls, who described a very useful concept, "the veil of ignorance," which refers to a heuristic exercise that attempts to control for knowledge of where one is in the social order, and then suggests approaches for designing an optimally fair social order. We all have to answer this question ourselves, but if I had no idea where I was in the social order, I know that the potential exists that I would be a person in dire need of help. I would want those who by chance wound up in superior positions to be in possession of the most effective techniques for helping me. Rawls came to a similar conclusion and allows for unequal distribution of power and resources, provided the inequality serves the purposes of the person in the weaker position (e.g., a behavior analyst designing an environment to help another person learn to communicate).

The second individual discussed was Immanuel Kant, and his argument that persons must be treated as ends unto themselves.

This captures the practice of behavior analysis quite well. Each person is treated as a separate entity, and the maximum benefit that can be derived for the individual is striven for. Nice sounding arguments about human worth and dignity don't cut it when confronted with a person who truly needs serious help. If an individual cannot communicate, feed him/herself, or even toilet independently, then high-sounding discussions of freedom, individual worth, and human potential sound somewhat empty. I think it more moral to use a technology that teaches behavior that allows for human dignity than to allow people to remain in a state of helplessness or degradation while assuring them that they are being treated morally.

I have digressed into this discussion so that the interventions that were discussed above can be put into perspective without the shadow of this question of the morality of behavior analysis hanging over our heads. The studies mentioned are just a few of many that behavior analysts have been conducting over the last two decades. These interventions were designed because it was decided that problems existed (and still exist) in these (and other) areas. Behavior analysis can go a long way toward solving many problems, but before it can be applied, however, we must recognize that a problem exists in a given area and a goal or "target behavior" must be chosen. The philosophy of humanism allows us to examine various parts of our lives and to see if things are as we want them. If not, it suggests how to correct the situation. Behavior analysis can then help enact the solution.

4

Education for Humanist Goals

More and more these days, we hear that our schools are failing to teach students the skills necessary to become productive members of society. If this is indeed the case (and there is some evidence that it is—Wyatt [1990]), then clearly there is something wrong in our massive educational establishment. Some critics have suggested that the problem is located in one or another particular area and is simply a matter of one or more individuals in the education establishment not being capable of doing their jobs, or possibly the presence of some situational factor that prevents the jobs from getting done. Such "localist" views place the blame on many different heads within the educational establishment (Vargas 1988). The key to solving our education problems, according to this localist "fix it" model, is to cure the problem area. The localists advocate changes in accordance with where they place the blame. Alternately, it has been suggested that perhaps the established power in our country does not want a society whose members can think for themselves; are intelligent and informed consumers; do not give in to religious authority; or accept politicians who are skilled at smiling, waving, and spouting rhetoric, but who are rather inefficient at problem solving (e.g., Sagan [1987]). According to this generalist "they don't want to fix it" model, the whole system needs an overhaul. Which of these conceptions is correct will be left to the individual to decide and advocates of either theory will find support in this chapter.

All too often we use the schools as a cop-out. Have a problem with drugs? Teach drug prevention in the schools! Have a problem with "x, y, or z"? Teach "x, y, or z" in the schools! Before we lay the responsibility for our social problems on the schools, we would do well to more clearly define the role of our schools. Should their primary goal be making good citizens, perpetuating the culture, serving the government, teaching some ideology, imparting facts, or teaching behavior codes? We could probably find advocates of all these ideas; some would even suggest that the schools should do all this and more.

We cannot expect the schools to do more than they are capable of. They are agents of socialization to be sure, but we cannot expect them to teach any behavior that would not be supported by the outside environment (see Cohen and Filipczak, chapter 3). Students experience life outside the classroom. They know what reality is; they experience it. I think we all remember well the lessons we were taught in school about how we were supposed to behave in "real life" and what the consequences of this behavior would be. By the time I reached junior high school I, and all but the most sheltered of people I knew, responded to such lessons with "spare me." I don't think I was unnecessarily cynical, and I certainly didn't have the reason to be that many other students did. It is foolish to expect some object lesson (designed to impart, for example, "crime doesn't pay," "you're only fooling yourself," "honesty is the best policy," "there are scholarships and opportunities that are unclaimed every year," "acting outrageously is not the way to get attention," "all people are created equal," and any one of a thousand similar lessons) to leave a lasting impression when the realities of the real world do not support them.

Advocates of "humanistic education" (seemingly of "third force" humanism) believe that the problem of teaching basic skills versus object lessons should become a nonissue. This can be accomplished if the schools accept "the self" as a subject to be taught. Swell, in her *Enhancing the Self: Techniques for Teachers* (1974, p. 2) makes the following observation:

Why . . . are curriculums centered on subject matter still being pushed by our most prominent educators as the be-all and end-all of education to the exclusion of the development of the self? "Humanistic education" is the beginning of what has got to be the most important trend in modern education. It would be foolish to say that the traditional subjects of reading, writing and 'rithmetic should be eliminated from the classroom and no one has suggested that, but if education is indeed a preparation for life then it would be a serious crime of omission to neglect the self as a subject to be taught.

The techniques she describes are designed to be used when teaching standard subject material, and are designed to (p. 4):

1. help the student become aware of himself;

2. help students become aware of each other;

3. help further the teachers' understanding of the students;

4. help both teachers and students actualize their awareness.

Through this process of "self and other" discovery, students learn not only basic skills, but more importantly, to develop their own talents in this age of technological advancement (where school-learned skills can become obsolete in a matter of months or years). They also seek to give the student the confidence to develop as a person. This love of self-esteem is a double-edged sword. On the one hand, researchers such as Bandura (1986) have suggested that those who have a realistic belief in their ability to cope in a given situation ("self-efficacy") tend to be more effective in those situations and also to suffer less anxiety and depression. On the other hand, for example, students in the United States rank themselves highest on self-assessment of math skills, while scoring lowest on tests of math ability (Wyatt 1990). Do we want students who feel good about themselves, or those who actually master the skills? As we will see, we can have both.

As with the third force psychotherapists, the third force educators have chosen goals in keeping with their perception (or preconceived notion) of perfect humanity. As with the third force psychotherapists, there is nothing necessarily humanistic about their point of view, no more so than most education theorists could claim. Like their psychotherapeutic counterparts, third force educators believe results (rather than process) oriented, often behaviorally based, approaches to teaching are misguided. On the other side, educators concerned with imparting basic skills regard this third force viewpoint as "misplaced humanism," and state: "It is one thing to express concern. It's another to *do* something about it" (Englemann, as quoted in Binder and Watkins 1989, p. 38). Just as Skinner insisted that behaviorism had the distinction of being effective humanism, Binder and Watkins contend that "effective instructional methods are effective humanism" (ibid.).

The goals to which we should extend this promised, and later to be proven, effective instruction must still be decided. Extrapolating from the statement of humanist philosophy offered in chapter one, the first job of the schools is to impart the knowledge and skills necessary for the student to become a productive member of society. In addition to its traditional meaning, *productive* here also refers to imparting the skills in reasoning, science, and knowledge-gathering that allow the individual to fully participate in our democracy. The schools must teach basic knowledge ("the three Rs" and the basics of such other subject areas as history, anthropology, geography, sexuality, and the various areas of science). They must teach research and reasoning processes, and impart the confidence necessary for young people to believe that the conclusions they have arrived at are valid. If we can acknowledge these as acceptable goals for the schools, the object then becomes one of finding a way to achieve them. How should the schools do their work? To answer this question, we must look at Project Follow-Through.

PROJECT FOLLOW-THROUGH

(Note: this section is based almost entirely on articles which appeared in the July/August 1988 issue of *Youth Policy,* particularly Watkins [1988].)

In the mid-1960s, the Head Start education project began in the United States. Head Start was an early education program designed to aid the poverty-stricken to break out of the poverty cycle by helping them to get an education and learn marketable skills. Head Start was hailed as a great educational boost to socio-economically disadvantaged youth. Subsequent research, however, suggested that the gains of Head Start students were lost when the children entered normal school programs. To maintain these gains it was decided that the program would have to be extended into the elementary school system.

Project Follow-Through was conceived as the carry-through program. Unfortunately, a budget cut led to the conversion of this program into a massive research project regarding the most effective means of education. Fifty-one school districts were selected to participate in the study. Several different educational strategies were tested across these settings. The first group of approaches was known as the "Basic Skills" group, and included *Direct Instruction, Behavior Analysis,* and the *Language Development Approach* (a bilingual strategy for Spanish speaking students). This first group focused primarily on the teaching of fundamental skills. The second set of approaches, known as the "Cognitive-Conceptual" group, included *Florida Parent Education, Tucson Early Education,* and the *Cognitively Oriented Curriculum.* These methods sought to develop "learning-to-learn" and problem-solving skills. The third group consisted of "Affective-Cognitive" approaches, which included *Responsive Education, Bank Street,* and *Open Education.* These models focused on developing positive self-concepts and attitudes toward learning and also learning-to-learn skills.

The first finding of Project Follow-Through should come as no surprise: the models that focused on teaching basic skills were more effective in this task than the other approaches. On measures of basic skills, the Direct Instruction and Behavior Analysis methods were the only ones that posted positive results. Because these methods were the ones proven most effective, they warrant some description. The Direct Instruction method emphasizes that all children can be taught, that basic skills are essential to higher-order thinking and should be a focus of a compensatory education program, and that disadvantaged children must be taught at a faster rate so as to catch up with their middle-class peers (Carnine 1988). Direct Instruction also has a strong behavioral component featuring the individualistic, results-oriented approach characteristic of behavior analysis. Behavior analysis in the education system (as described by Dorow [1988]) capitalizes on all the advantages of its single-subject research methodology described earlier (see also the quotes from Bijou below). It provides children with continuous opportunities to engage in academic tasks, provides valid instructional material programmed in carefully researched and designed sequential steps, provides continuous immediate feedback for responses, mixes in previously learned material with new material, and teaches until the material is mastered. Progress is continuously measured and reviewed.

The second finding may be a bit surprising. Students taught by models that emphasized something other than basic skills tended to score *lower* on tests of basic skills than they would have had they had no Project Follow-Through exposure. In effect, with the exception of Direct Instruction and Behavior Analysis, the Project Follow-Through programs exacerbated the very problems they were designed to solve. On tests of cognitive-conceptual abilities no model was notably more successful than the others, despite the fact that some of the models tested were designed for this very purpose.

As regards the self-efficacy dilemma mentioned above, we happily find no conflict. The methods that taught basic skills— i.e., Direct Instruction and Behavior Analysis—also posted the best results when measuring student self-concept (again, despite the fact that the group of models tested were designed for this very purpose). It seems that rather than being a prerequisite for learning, self-concept is a by-product of actually mastering skills.

Unfortunately for students, the government response to these findings was disheartening, to say the least. Although the expressed purpose of Project Follow-Through was to identify and disseminate effective educational technology, this task was not met. The offices charged with disseminating the results of the study identified twenty-two programs as exemplary. Among the programs validated as "exemplary" were those that failed to improve academic achievement. The idea was expressed that the office had to be "fair" and represent the multiplicity of methods in education. Being fair to the students and giving them what they deserve—effective instruction—was apparently not considered. A second discouraging fallout regards the funding of programs. Higher levels of funding have been allocated to programs that were not validated, despite the fact that evidence suggests that increased financial support will not improve the efficacy of ineffective programs. Further, rather than following up on methods that were proven effective, more money has been spent in the attempt to study new approaches. The key question of these new studies is "whether or not an approach can be put into place and maintained, not with the effectiveness of the approach in improving student outcomes" (Proper and St. Pierre, quoted in Watkins [1988, p. 10]).

Why this should be the case was addressed by Watkins (ibid.), who characterizes the education establishment:

> As in other bureaucracies, it is composed of parochial vested interests that work either to preserve the status quo or to advance a self-serving agenda. The educational establishment's vested interests have effectively prevented the largest experiment in history on instructional methods (costing almost one billion dollars) from having the impact on daily classroom practice that its results clearly warranted.

The current education establishment is not prepared for the techniques that have clearly been proven effective. Few teachers have been trained in Behavior Analysis or in Direct Instruction. If the findings of Project Follow-Through were implemented, a whole generation of educational administrators would find themselves untrained for their own positions. This point is expanded upon by Cook (1988, p. 3):

> Serious resistance to powerful instructional methods is to be found within the educational establishment itself. . . . This resistance seems not to be altered even when the objective scientific data is presented which documents the superiority of a particular method. Interests are threatened, or are perceived to be in danger. It must be acknowledged that new methods of instruction will probably require adjustments in the current career structure of the teaching profession, and make unfamiliar demands upon those who would stay in this field.

The losers in this political mess are, of course, the students and the general public. They engage in endless debates focusing on everything but the key issue:

> The general public has no way of knowing that children's achievements are largely a function of the instructional methods used by their teachers. . . . Endless studies and reports call attention to important factors such as improving curricula, increasing teacher salaries, expanding the length of the school day and/or year and a variety of other changes. Although these changes are probably desirable, they will not be sufficient to produce the substantial academic improvement that has been shown to be possible. The critical factor that has been consistently ignored is instructional method. The educational problems of this country are unlikely to be fully solved until it is recognized that how well students learn is more a function of how they are taught than any other factor. (Watkins, p. 11)

This is all in the recent past. For the future, Shanley (1988, p. 28) advises,

> We have two choices. We can continue to waste monies by putting them into programs that are ineffective and into more studies that provide the same information already collected in the past. Or, we can spend our efforts and monies on improving programs already in existence.

Project Follow-Through demonstrated that effective teaching programs are available and that teachers can be trained to use these programs effectively. It also demonstrated the enormous political red tape that surrounds our education system, and suggests that these political forces do not necessarily have the best interests of students at heart. Like other bureaucracies, it has become self-perpetuating. For as long as those who make the decisions regarding education policy in our country continue to ignore the results of Project Follow-Through, our schools will probably continue to receive failing grades.

WHAT OF CREATIVITY?

Perhaps by now the point would be conceded that behaviorist instruction can impart basic skills efficiently, and this instruction leads to better self-image than techniques that have this as a primary goal. A final consideration would be this: if behavioral interventions are efficient at imparting already known knowledge, then what of as-yet unknown knowledge? Wouldn't a behavioral approach stifle the creativity of the student? (Remember Kohlberg's characterization of "student-proof" teaching from chapter three.) Happily, the answer is no. Although this concept may be counterintuitive, creativity itself can be taught.

We generally regard characteristics such as "creativity" as something that a person either has or does not have (hence the semireligious characterization of a "gift"). Yet another piece of research that is nearly two decades old questions this conception. Research conducted by Goetz and Baer (1973) examined the behavior of preschool children and suggested that, rather than being some vague and esoteric entity, creativity is something that can be taught.

Goetz and Baer examined a behavior that is common in the preschool setting: block building. Three students were identified by the staff as particularly deficient in creativity with regard to block building. Baseline observations of the children confirmed this impression. Only a few variations in design of block structures were observed. Goetz and Baer decided to treat "creativity" like any other behavior. They instituted a behavioral intervention to increase the diversity of block patterns, reinforcing with praise when a block pattern previously unattempted by the child was created. The diversity of observed forms then increased dramatically. Suddenly, through the use of a structured environment, the children no longer "lacked creativity." The researchers then reversed the intervention and only reinforced previously seen patterns. "Creativity" then dropped to levels comparable to baseline. In the final reversal, the researchers again reinforced diversity in form. The number of original variations again increased significantly.

Too often, our education system pigeon-holes students and attributes their behavior and accomplishments to some stable and internal characteristic. As with Project Follow-Through regarding academic achievement, different "talents" are susceptible to change through the use of behavioral science. Perhaps none of the children studied grew up to be a great artist or architect. Perhaps that talent is something one must be born with, although no one has ever proven this common belief. But that is not the point. Autocracy can be taught, but so can autonomy. We can reinforce, and by definition encourage, the ability to question what exists and to improve upon it. If education is indeed a subversive activity—and I believe it should be—then we can use effective teaching methods to encourage social progress. University courses that taught the basic skill of critical thinking were effective in reducing belief in popular myths (Gray 1984, Tobacyk 1983, Woods 1984). Teaching students to examine prevailing beliefs should prove no less successful.

Earlier, we examined Carl Rogers and his idea of unconditional positive regard as a necessary condition for personal growth. Advocates of many "third force" schools of education have expressed the same idea. Through unconditional positive regard (noncontingent reinforcement) individuals develop the confidence to grow and assert their own ideas. This would seem to run counter to what we have discussed. It does. Earlier we pointed out how both naturalistic humanism and behavior analysis are anxiety-provoking because they challenge some of our most comforting notions. This idea of unconditional positive regard as an essential component for growth is, unfortunately, one belief which must fall. Noncontingent reinforcement, even if delivered in abundance, will not encourage desired behavior (as demonstrated with regard to cooperation by Hart, Reynolds, Baer, Brawley, and Harris [1968]). If a particular behavior is desirable, that behavior, and not it's antithesis, should be reinforced. Despite our romantic notions, there is still no virtue in accident.

SELF-MANAGEMENT

All this talk of structured environments may seem counter-intuitive. The concept of free will is quite pervasive, and for good reason (Lamont 1982). We have a conscious awareness of choosing our actions. Couldn't we avoid a great many of the problems for which behavioral solutions have been implemented simply by developing the individual's power or desire to choose the desirable behavior? While it is contrary to what we have discussed to look to an autonomous inner being for control of behavior, there is an area of research, ironically named "self-management," that is relevant here and answers this question in the affirmative.

Skinner (1953) is generally cited as the first individual to describe self-management, i.e., the attempt to apply operant principles to one's own behavior. Although Skinner originally named this area "self-control," his term has led to some philosophical confusion, e.g., regarding whether the locus of control of behavior is actually within the individual (the "self") or within the environment, as is more commonly believed (Cooper, Heron, and Heward 1987, pp. 515-18). "Self-management" is the preferred term for this set of procedures, for two reasons. First, the term does not as strongly suggest control by an autonomous inner being, and second, it eliminates the confusion between the type of "self-control" behavior management strategy described by Skinner (1953, pp. 227-41) and the "self-control" (delay of gratification) process described by Rachlin and Green (1972).

Even with this confusion eliminated, some researchers (e.g., Catania 1975 and Goldiamond 1976) have charged that the whole area of self-management is a mass of logical contradictions. Contending that self-reinforcement (and related terms) are misnomers, these authors cite the fact that increases in probability of behavior that define reinforcement are not always present (thus the process of reinforcement is not being accurately depicted by the term), that it is not really the "self" that is being observed (or reinforced) but rather some behavior of the organism (thus Catania's suggestion that self-awareness is actually the subject matter, and his insistence that two behaviors—the target behavior and the behavior of self-delivery of reinforcement—are in question), and that the judgment as to whether the response has met criteria for reinforcement is, in all cases except "self-reinforcement," generally made from without rather than by the "self" (the decision to reinforce is not independent of organism, as insisted upon particularly by Goldiamond). Most seriously, Catania and Goldiamond fear that self-reinforcement might too easily become an explanatory fiction. Invoking self-management might thus halt the search for the real contingencies affecting behavior, which are likely to be found outside the individual "self-managing" organism.

Despite these philosophical difficulties, self-management techniques have been successfully employed in a variety of settings (e.g., Broden, Hall, and Mitts 1971, Harris 1986, McFall 1977, O'Leary and Dubey 1979, Richman et al. 1988, Rosenbaum and

Drabman 1979). Koegel and Koegel (1990) describe several advantages to teaching self-management skills. First, self-management may be used over long periods in the absence of a trainer. Second, self-management skills can be adapted to a variety of settings and behavior. The virtues of self-management training were expanded upon by Cooper, Heron, and Heward (1987, p. 518). Instances of important behavior change might be missed by external agents but not by the individual; certain types of behavior (e.g., smoking, exercise, assertiveness) do not lend themselves to external-agent control; those with self-management skills require less trainer time; self-management can be used to control behavior not affected by weak or distant outcomes; some people perform better under self-selected standards; and finally, self-management "feels good." Interestingly, many of these advantages mirror those outlined by Karen Horney (1942) with regard to another form of "self analysis."

Self-management is a skill that can be taught, much like any other. That it is not taught in the schools is something of a mystery. According to Cooper, Heron, and Heward (p. 520):

> John Dewey (1939) . . . said that "the ideal aim of education is the creation of self-control" (p. 75). A student's ability to be self-directed, with the teacher as guide or facilitator, and his ability to self-evaluate his performance are . . . cornerstones of a humanistic education. (Gage and Berliner 1975)

When taught self-management skills, people learn diverse skills for making desired behavior more probable. This can take the form of self-recording (e.g., counting the number of cigarettes smoked in a day. Self-monitoring may also lead to "reactivity," a change in the behavior due only to the act of recording it as in McFall [1977]), setting consequences for one's own behavior (e.g., contracting with another to give your money to a hated organization if you do not complete a given piece of work in a given time), or creating an environment that makes certain behavior either more or less probable (e.g., not bringing sweets into the house when dieting). These "self-chosen" interventions can be just as effective as those chosen by others, and can sometimes be even more effective. They also have an advantage in that

achieving behavior change through these means is itself reinforcing (Malott 1981, cited in Cooper, Heron, and Heward 1987,
p. 520).

Though these skills are collectively known as "self-management," the term is something of a misnomer. The locus of control
is not within the individual, but rather within the environment
designed by the individual. This self-management behavior is itself
under the control of environmental consequences (e.g., the reinforcement of losing weight and the social reinforcers this entails).
Self-management training has been successfully applied to academic
tasks (e.g., Cossairt, Hall, and Hopkins 1973; Drabman and Lahey
1974; Kneedler and Hallahan 1981; Van Houten, Morrison, Jarvis,
and McDonald 1974). Students have been taught, for example,
to monitor and reinforce their own on-task time and even accuracy
in carrying out tasks. Self-management training should be an aspect
of any education effort; someone else may not always be available
to help the individual to keep up with desirable, but often tedious,
academic tasks. Self-management training ensures that someone
will always be there.

IMPLEMENTING HUMANIST EDUCATION

I was once engaged in a conversation with a woman who objected
to the behavioral approach to education. In discussing the matter,
it turned out that this individual had been an elementary school
teacher for over twenty years. She had left the profession when
she could no longer accept the work of behaviorists practicing
in her classroom. What type of credentials or training the behaviorists had she could not say (remember the problem of
untrained "pseudo-behavior analysts" mentioned in chapter one).
She saw the behaviorists as bullies who had no conception of
what was really going on within the child. She told me the story
of what sounded like an inappropriate use of "time-out" (a procedure whereby a child is briefly removed from ongoing reinforcement contingent upon inappropriate behavior) as an example of
the horror. I attempted to explain that behavior analysis is a process
of examining the functional relationships of behavior, and not
just using techniques without monitoring results (as this practi-

tioner, whatever his or her real training and qualifications, apparently did). I also tried to explain that the person who performed this procedure did not follow ethical guidelines accepted by behavior analysts (see chapter three). I don't think my explanation carried much weight with her; she didn't seem at all convinced.

Probably the only way to avoid such negative experiences, which in this case unfortunately contributed to the termination of her career, is for behavior analysts to involve staff members in the planning of interventions and in the data collection and analysis process, and to always explain the rationale for what is being done. Staff compliance is likely to be heightened, and thus benefits from treatment will be more probable. Input from those familiar with the students will also be greater, and more efficient interventions may be suggested. The behavior analyst should not seek to "clean up the town" singlehanded. Such aggressive attempts are likely to lead to confusion and alienation from the rest of the staff, and therefore hinder work with the clients. That would be too bad, considering the good that could be done.

In an invited address delivered to the American Psychological Association's Division of School Psychologists, Sidney Bijou (1970) analyzed "what psychology has to offer education now." The behavior analysts, he said,

> can offer a set of concepts and principles derived exclusively from experimental research: we can offer a methodology for applying these concepts and principles directly to teaching practices; we can offer a research design which deals with changes in the individual child (rather than inferring them from group averages); and we can offer a philosophy of science which insists on observable accounts of the relationships between individual behavior and its determining conditions. (p. 66)

Bijou (p. 71) predicted that "the ultimate result, of course, would be a better educated community—the first requisite in equipping an industrial society to manage the advances of science and technology to achieve *humanitarian* goals." In view of what we have discussed above, this would seem to be what we have been striving to achieve.

5

The ABA, Humanism, and Public Policy

In the last section of *Behaviorism,* John B. Watson (1970/1924, pp. 303–304) wrote:

> I am trying to dangle a stimulus in front of you, a verbal stimulus which, if acted upon, will gradually change this universe. For this universe will change if you bring up your children, not in the freedom of the libertine, but in behavioristic freedom. . . . Will not these children, in turn, with their better ways of living and thinking, replace us as society and in turn bring up their children in a still more scientific way, until the world finally becomes a place fit for human habitation?

Despite this clear statement of his intentions, untrue rumors regarding Watson's life (and Skinner's, e.g., that he drove his children insane) are rampant in the literature regarding the history of psychology (Todd 1990), and thus we must take accounts of his private life with a large grain of salt. One fact that seems to be reasonably well established, however, is that Watson's own children were not particularly impressed with his ideas. It is said that one child even committed what we should probably regard as the ultimate insult to Watson by becoming a psychoanalyst (Duke,

Fried, Piley, and Walker 1989). It would be unfair, however, to blame this hostility on behavior analysis. The blame must instead be placed on Watson himself, his failure to understand the difference between behavior analysis as description and as prescription (a mistake similar to that of Maslow), his failure to appreciate the contingencies to which his children would be exposed outside his home (see *A New Learning Environment* and *A Clockwork Orange,* chapter 3), and his failure to acknowledge the limits of his system (which at this point had not yet embraced operant technology).

A theme running throughout this work has been that behavior analysis cannot decide which behavior to encourage and thus requires an outside framework to guide applications. It has been my suggestion that humanism is the philosophy best suited to provide this framework. Before we look at current ideas as to where applications are needed and how effective applications have been, we shall examine the work of Auguste Comte and his efforts in this direction.

AUGUSTE COMTE

How much influence the work of Auguste Comte (1798-1857), the "father of positivism," has had in the development of behavior analysis is something of a controversy. On the one hand, writers such as Leahey (1987) characterize Skinner's ideas regarding the use of behavior analysis on the societal level as nothing more than "secular Comtism." On the other hand, Watson's 1913 article, "Psychology as the Behaviorist Views It," is usually cited as the first milestone in behavior analysis. An informal survey I conducted on Compuserve's Behavioral Bulletin Board (the telecomputer outlet of the International Association for Behavior Analysis) revealed that none of the participants had ever seen Comte's name mentioned in a book written by behavior analysts about their field. The point has been raised that it is very improbable that the writings of Comte, a French philosopher, would have been read by the German and American scientists who laid the framework for behavior analysis. Leahey, however, suggests that Comte's thought inspired people throughout Europe and that the positivist movement became especially influential in the philosophy of science. He names Claude Bernard and Ernest Mach, the latter of whom is named by Skinner as a major influence, as two individuals particularly influenced by positivist thought. We can therefore probably accept Comte's influence, albeit perhaps indirect, in the development of applied behavior analysis. (The fact that Comte may not be given credit for his influence may spring from some of his behavior in the last years of his life. As mentioned in chapter one, Comte formed a ritual-laden "positivistic church," with his deceased young mistress serving as something of a patron saint to this Religion of Humanity. Comte also attempted suicide on more than one occasion, and it has been suggested that his later writings displayed some elements of paranoia [Aiken 1956]. The failure to acknowledge his influence may represent an avoidance of the conflicts that would necessarily arise in separating his earlier work from his later, perhaps insane, writings.)

Comte's thought can probably best be conceptualized as an attempt to make a complete break with Idealistic philosophy, which still clung to certain elements of the Christian viewpoint that held so much influence in medieval times. By Comte's time the Christian world-view had been seriously questioned. A new system was needed from which a new world-view could be synthesized. Following Saint-Simon (1760–1825), Comte's thought represents an attempt to make positivism, his view of the methods of science, this system.

According to Comte, human thought (both individual and societal) could be viewed as an inevitable progression through three stages, which he collectively named the "Law of Human Progress." If we look at the developed areas of human inquiry (those which have reached the positivistic stage), according to Comte, we will always find that they passed through the two previous stages.

The first of these stages is the Theological, where anthropomorphism is the rule. Natural phenomena are regarded as the immediate actions of supernatural beings, and everything is endowed with a purpose, will, or spirit. The apex of this stage of thought is when one sentient god takes on the role previously assigned to many gods. Interestingly, Comte suggested that it is the grandiosity of this stage (a belief that humans are important enough for supernatural beings to be so concerned with our affairs) that gives the impetus for the questioning that must lead to the next two stages.

The second phase that must inevitably be passed through is the Metaphysical, where, instead of sentient supernatural beings, the "essences," "tendencies," or "natures" of things are held to be responsible for natural phenomena. Instead of a sentient god, the necessary "first cause" of this stage takes on an impersonal nature and is no longer locatable in any specific phenomena. Explanations in this phase consist of deductive proofs from self-evident truths. Controversies that must inevitably break out regarding these "self-evident" truths signal the end of this stage of thought.

The third stage, which Comte considered the apex of human thought, is the Positivistic. In this mature phase, the controversies of the Theological and Metaphysical stages are dismissed as futile and useless. Knowledge is based only on observable relationships among phenomena. These observable relationships are then classified into general laws, which allow for the description, prediction, and control of phenomena to the benefit of humanity. The aim of this final stage is to reduce the number of laws that govern these observable relationships.

The sciences, according to Comte, reach the positivistic stage at rates that differ depending upon many factors, including their simplicity and dependence on the other sciences. Mathematics was the first area of inquiry to mature. It was followed by astronomy, terrestrial physics, chemistry, physiology, and finally "social physics." Comte coined the term "sociology" to describe social physics, and admitted that at his time it had not yet been seriously attempted.

Conspicuous by its absence from Comte's hierarchy is psychology, which he considered a discipline from an immature stage of thought. (Watson's equation of introspective psychology with religion, or a prescientific view, mirrors this notion.) To Comte, psychology was broken down into two disciplines, phrenology (an attempt to relate specific personality characteristics to specific brain areas) and sociology (functional relationships among the observable phenomena that govern behavior). In modern terms, psychology has been broken down into our current areas of neuropsychology and behavior analysis. Comte was so convinced that introspective psychology was a useless pursuit that he wrote:

The results of such a method (introspection) are in proportion to its absurdity. After 2,000 years of psychological pursuit, no one proposition is established to the satisfaction of its followers. (Comte, quoted in Aiken 1956, p. 133)

If there is any doubt that Comte is an intellectual forerunner of Skinner, one need only read the opening chapter of *Beyond Freedom and Dignity,* wherein Skinner wrote (p. 3):

Twenty-five hundred years ago it might have been said that man understood himself as well as any other part of his world. . . . Greek physics and biology are now of historical interest only (no modern physicist would turn to Aristotle for help), but the dialogues of Plato are still assigned to students and cited as if they threw light on human behavior.

Interestingly, some behavior analysts no longer consider themselves psychologists. They reason that the methods and subject matter of behavior analysis (i.e., a concern with the functional relationships of behavior) are so different from those of psychologists (e.g., a concern with undemonstrable, unconscious conflicts; cognitions as ends unto themselves; testing meant to demonstrate [often symbolically] nebulous concepts such as "intelligence" or "personality"; or universal stages of psychological development separate and apart from environmental influences) that a new discipline, behaviorology, should be recognized. As psychology split from philosophy in the late 1800s, so might we eventually see behaviorology split from psychology.

It might be suspected from Comte's tough-minded view of human progress that he was something of a stern intellectual. He was actually an idealistic social reformer. His primary audiences were women and working people, those he felt were oppressed by the then (and probably currently) prevailing social contingencies. His positivistic church was an attempt to spread his gospel that the methods of science, properly applied, could provide answers to the many problems facing society at the time, suggest the path to Order and Progress, and provide the basis by which Love and Service to one's fellow citizens could become possible as a way of life. To these ends, a group of experts in sociology would eventually come to design society and their ideas would be accepted by the masses because of the experts' demonstrated abilities.

Unfortunately, Comte is often dismissed as a thinker. This might be the result of knee-jerk negative reactions to notions of society based on determinism (see chapter 1). Also, the best features of Comte's thought have been lost in the controversy regarding his mental state, his expert-ruled society, and the distaste that many intellectuals hold for his ritual-laden positivistic church (Aiken 1956). Nonetheless, what Comte suggested is in the finest traditions of both behavior analysis and humanism. His "experts" use the methods of science in an attempt to understand behavior and try to use this knowledge to realize goals that would have to be regarded as humanistic.

BEHAVIOR ANALYSIS IN THE COMMUNITY

Is this what behavior analysts would like to see: a utopia/dystopia where behaviorally trained experts design our lives? Based upon the literature of behavior analysis, as opposed to that of its critics (e.g., Carpenter 1974), I think we can rest assured that its goal is nothing so drastic or frightening. Rather than the institution of some overall system, the behavioral approach to society is a situation-analysis approach that can and should be applied to the goals suggested by humanist philosophy (a situation-specific, first-order change rather than a more global second-order societal change—Fawcett, Mathews, and Fletcher [1980]). The behavior analyst may indeed design policy, not as a tyrant but rather as a "partner and colleague in social reform. Our role in the change process will be as a catalyst—to assist in the design of solutions" (Holland 1978, p. 173).

Examples of work done by behavior analysts over the last twenty years—work that addresses many different social problems—are collected in an excellent volume edited by Greene, Winett, Van Houten, Geller, and Iwata (1987), which brings together some fifty-four articles published in the *Journal of Applied Behavior Analysis*. The articles are gathered under several general headings: general and conceptual issues, crime prevention and intervention, preserving the ecology, promoting pro-social behavior in the

community, promoting safety, evaluation of social and governmental programs, citizen and consumer affairs, and applications
regarding employment and business practices. The interventions
described in these studies follow the pattern of behavior analytic
studies described earlier: a problem is recognized; the behavior
which contributes to this problem is measured (baseline); an
intervention is then implemented (experimental phase) and the
results measured. Various procedures may be tried in an attempt
to discover the crucial variables that control the behavior. In this
way, cost-effective and efficient methods are found for carrying
out social policy goals.

Unfortunately, the findings of such behavioral studies are only
rarely implemented (with notable exceptions, e.g., the refuse collection program of Stokes and Fawcett [1977]). There are several
reasons for this failure, the first being that special-interest groups
may resist the changes (as with the education studies). Also, many
behavioral studies are conducted by academics, individuals who
suffer from the pressure of "publish or perish" (Diamond 1989),
and this prevents many studies from being anything more than
"publishable" short-term demonstration projects. Problems with
experimental design also make it difficult for standard behavior
analytic research (e.g., single-subjects and nonstatistical data analysis) to be employed, and the effects of these interventions have
often been short-lived with little generalization. Such problems are
being addressed, and studies have begun to change for the better
(Geller 1987). Problems do not always go away just because we
know what must be done. A mouse with complete knowledge
of behavior would still, due to lack of control over contingencies,
be in no position to shape complex behavior. In order to change
behavior, we have to put our knowledge into practice, and there
are often obstacles in the way, including "common sense."

Let us take, for example, a study conducted by Bacon-Prue,
Blount, Pickering, and Drabman (1980). The researchers noted
that litter was a problem in a residence for the developmentally
disabled. There being no trash receptacles available, the researchers
placed receptacles on the grounds and continued to monitor litter
levels. The litter level did not drop significantly. The researchers
then hired a number of supervised residents to serve as trash
collectors. Again, the litter problem was not significantly abated.

The researchers then began covertly marking (with a spray that would only show up under ultraviolet light) certain pieces of litter and announced that rewards would be given to those who collected marked pieces of litter. For the first time, there was an abatement of the trash problem. A withdrawal of this program led to an increase in the level of litter on the grounds. A return to the marked item program saw another decrease in the level of litter.

A valid criticism is that this project was undertaken in a relatively isolated environment, an institution for the developmentally disabled. The "outside world" would certainly be different and such a procedure might be difficult to implement. What this study does suggest, however, is that some of our common-sense notions regarding problem solving may be off-base. Originally, there were no receptacles available. Conventional wisdom would say "put receptacles where people can see and use them, and the problem will disappear." It didn't work that way. Conventional wisdom also says that "if you need a job done, you hire someone to do it." Again, it didn't work that way. Neither common sense solution solved the problem. The procedure that took advantage of reinforcement did achieve results. This is in contrast to our societal consequences regarding littering (and most other areas of social conduct), which are almost always aversive (i.e., fines and imprisonment). As mentioned in chapter 1, behaviorally oriented social policy design relies much more on reinforcement than on punishment; "catch 'em being good," as the slogan goes.

The field of behavioral community psychology offers many exciting possibilities regarding social policy. For example, would it be possible to take advantage of the popularity of lotteries by making chances in the lottery contingent on some behavior other than putting down a dollar? The possibilities are exciting, particularly considering the amount of resources we currently expend in attempting to enforce aversive contingencies.

EXAMINING CURRENT SOCIAL POLICY

At this point, I must retreat from my preface promise to avoid disclaimers and state that the conclusions of the next two sections are exclusively my own. The reception these ideas have received from behavior analysts has been, at best, mixed. They are not to be interpreted as indicative of the viewpoint of behavior analysis or any organization that endorses such analysis. Because the data of this research are nonexperimental and general, the conclusions must be acted on carefully. The way to proceed with these analyses is in the way characteristic of behavioral interventions: i.e., *pilot studies which can be expanded upon if the results warrant, or altered if they prove counterproductive.* These views were written for a behavioral audience. To contrast how the behavior analyst and humanist might attack these problems, the topics were addressed in *Free Inquiry* magazine in the fall of 1989 and the spring of 1990. Versions of these two sections appeared in volume 1 of the journal *Behavior and Social Issues* (*1* [1] pp. 43-55 and *1* [2] pp. 15-24). My intention is to show how an appreciation of behavioral research and the behavioral framework might allow us to design data-based social policy.

POLITICAL IDEOLOGY

November 12, 1989, was a big day for the pro-choice forces in the abortion struggle. A few hundred thousand people poured into the U.S. capital to proclaim their (in my opinion, righteous) support for a woman's right to choose what should happen to her body. While walking in the crowd, I came across a table with a banner proclaiming "We're pro-choice everything!" That tolerant bunch turned out to be the Libertarian political party. Just to the right of this was another table, staffed by the Young Socialists.

There are libertarians who claim that individual rights begin at conception. There are also socialists who believe that "cradle to grave" should actually extend from "conception to grave." The majority opinion in both camps seems to be pro-choice. I thought it interesting that people with such disparate political ideologies could find an issue upon which they agreed in the basic idea, if not in the details and justifications (e.g., how abortions should be funded, why anti-abortion laws are unacceptable). The debates between libertarians (who are really radical capitalists—Rothbard [1978]) and socialists are fascinating and voluminous, each attempting to prove their system to be superior through the use of historical and current examples, as well as appeals to ideology. Ideology is defined here as behavior, in this case verbal behavior, which conforms to a set of rules considered correct and unchanging. So considered, the rules do not allow for the testing of interventions central to applied behavior analysis and are therefore undesirable.

In the "Socialism and Behaviorism" debate (*Behavior Analysis and Social Action*, 6(2): 16-32; 7: 23-34) Rakos, Morrow, and Ulman examine socialism and capitalism, and attempt to explain from a behavioral perspective why one system or the other is to be preferred. In so doing, the authors forgot one of the basic tenets of behavior analysis—treat each problem as a separate entity and do not assume that what is effective in one setting will necessarily prove effective in another. If behavior analysis is to give us any insight into designing social policy, then we must carefully define our problems and avoid making sweeping statements. Each problem area must be treated individually. This does not mean, however, that the wider context must be ignored (see Wahler and Fox 1981). Rather, it should not be assumed that any global policy (including socialism or capitalism) is likely to function as a panacea. To cavalierly implement a global intervention without an examination of the contingencies affecting the behavior at issue is not consistent with applied behavior "analysis." No political stance other than a willingness to analyze the contingencies of each individual problem area is likely to lead to successful solutions. This empirical stance conforms closely to the point of view known as "pragmatism" (Ulman, personal communication, 1990). Although the term "pragmatism" has been used in many ways, it is here used to define a belief that policies should not be "judged by their intrinsic righteousness or truth but, instead, should be evaluated in terms of their consequences" (Kendler 1987, p. 129). More than any other guiding philosophy, this idea seems to be compatible with the standard practice of setting a behavioral goal that is expected to maximize future reinforcement and then evaluating interventions in terms of whether or not the behavioral goals were reached (and not in terms of any other conception of "truthfulness"). It could be argued that this pragmatic viewpoint also constitutes an ideology and is, for the reason mentioned above, therefore undesirable.

If pragmatic empiricism is an ideology, it is one only in the broadest sense (the unchanging rule being that all policies must be open to question). Because of its adaptability, and its failure to block the testing of assertions—it actually demands such tests—this guiding philosophy would seem to be compatible with applied behavior analysis.

THE ENVIRONMENT

One of the most inspiring endings to a novel that I've ever read was that of *Anthem,* Ayn Rand's troubling vision of a socialist world. At the end of the novel, protagonist Equality 7-2521 (then renamed Prometheus) reclaims the individuality lost to humanity when the collectivist revolution occurred. He also begins to recreate the Genesis myth, reclaiming the dominion of humanity over the world's resources and creatures.

The results of human dominion over the earth and its creatures should not be news to anyone. Extinctions of animal and plant species have been widespread (e.g., Mowat 1986) and continue at an accelerating pace. The rain forests of the world are disappearing, leading to further extinctions and possibly global climatic changes (Caufield 1984, Forsyth and Miyata 1984). The hole in the ozone layer, resource shortages, and toxic waste are just a few consequences of the indiscriminate exploitation of nature by humankind and a lack of concern for the environmental impact of the choices we make. The libertarian position on the environment—that no government has the right to interfere with the individual's right to use available resources (as described in Agras, Jacob, and Lebedeck 1980, for example)—is thus probably not acceptable to anyone concerned with the continuing quality of life on the planet.

Our indiscriminate abuse of resources (e.g., Milleman 1986) and our failure to respond to the results of this abuse are predicted by Herrnstein's hyperbola and by the "choice behavior" literature. Briefly stated, Herrnstein contends that reinforcers must be considered relative to the density of all other reinforcers in the environment in order to predict their effects (McDowell 1982). Rachlin and Green's 1972 study of self-control suggests that organisms will prefer immediate reinforcers to temporally distant reinforcers, even if the latter are of greater magnitude than the immediate reinforcer (in accordance with the dimensions specified by a proportion known as the matching law). Similarly, Deluty (1978) found that temporally distant aversive stimuli will be preferred to more immediate aversive stimuli, even if the former is of greater magnitude than the latter. For the question of environmental preservation, the key point relating these studies is that the immediate reinforcement of consuming resources and disposing of the waste is too powerful to be countered by the temporally distant punishing contingencies (and many still consider this to be infinitely delayed) of an uninhabitable planet.

It may be that the recent concern with the environment (e.g., annual "Earth Day" programs) will lead to contingencies that favor environmental preservation. The power of consumers, for example, to favor environmentally responsible companies may alleviate some of the damage done by industry in the wealthier nations. This is unlikely to make a significant impact on the global scale, however. How long this concern will be in the public eye remains to be seen. How well industry may be able to hide its destructive practices is also unknown. Finally, in many countries there may be no incentive for industry to change its practices, and in the poorer nations there may be no choice but to continue environmentally destructive practices (e.g., deforestation to clear farm land for growing populations). Some form of government control on resource exploitation (e.g., the proposed multinational ban on resource exploitation in the Antarctic) is probably required if we are to prevent entering a time in which the aversive stimulation of an uninhabitable planet becomes more immediate and competitive with the reinforcement of consumption.

OVERPOPULATION

It was Parson Thomas Malthus (1766-1834) who popularized the point that human population increases at a faster rate than resources can be increased. The Club of Rome "think-tank" came to a confirmatory conclusion, stating that there are real limits to the growth of human population and resource consumption.

Despite the dangers of overpopulation and the problems inherent in a society that overpopulates, this trend continues in many countries (Fornos 1987, Mumford 1984). We can probably regard this trend as similar in nature to the trend of environmental destruction. The short-term reinforcers (for the individual, for government, for the church, or some other special interest group) of having children, be they social, economic, or intrinsic, are too powerful for the long-range punishers to compete.

As with the environmental crisis, this trend in the birthrate cannot continue forever. Eventually there will be an evening up of the contingencies. The key question comes down to the nature of the control mechanism involved. Should child-bearing be limited by society (a concept most would probably dislike), or should the crisis be allowed to reach a stage such that the aversive consequences of child-bearing become immediate (a concept most would probably like even less)? Rather than trusting political philosophies (both the socialists and the libertarians believe that their systems solve the population problem), we would be better off analyzing the contingencies of this problematic area (e.g., Cone and Hayes 1984) and designing social policy accordingly. It is my impression that the evidence favors the need for state intervention. This need not only take the form of limits on the number of children a given family can have (e.g., the Chinese effort to restrict families to one child). As pointed out by Fornos (1990), a great many women, particularly in the developing countries, would like to cease having children but lack the education or resources to realize this wish. (Adding to this problem, the United States government, pressured by "pro-life" forces, has cut its aid for voluntary family planning in developing countries). Rather than government intervention functioning to set guidelines for behavior, this area may require state intervention that makes adaptive behavior possible.

INDUSTRY

What it is that causes people to be truly productive was one of the main points of contention for Ulman (1988) and Rakos (1988a). Reading their articles, I was reminded of the contrast between Upton Sinclair's scathing view of capitalism in *The Jungle* and the previously mentioned and equally scathing view of socialism in Ayn Rand's *Anthem*. While neither Ulman nor Rakos went as far as the novelists did advocating their system and pointing out weaknesses in the opposing system, both looked at the same ideas and phenomena and came to radically different conclusions.

According to Rakos, the capitalist system is superior. He feels that the contingent relationship between work and obtaining material and subsequent social reinforcers is in keeping with a view of human nature as described by behavior analysis. Ulman takes issue with what he considers to be a bourgeois conception, questioning Rakos's analysis and the use of the term "human nature." Rakos (1988a, p. 16) himself acknowledges that "human nature" is an explanatory fiction, but nonetheless is willing to accept capitalism as consistent with an "operationalized conception of human nature" (p. 20). I think the evidence supports Rakos's view that there must be a contingent relationship between work and reinforcement, but I also agree with Ulman (p. 27) that the behavior we might attribute to "human nature," operationalized or not, is better conceptualized as being selected by its consequences. To say that one social system takes better advantage of this relationship is one thing; to say that the system is more consistent with human nature is quite another.

The poor state of the economies of the socialist countries would seem to suggest that socialism is not a very effective system with regard to industry, possibly for the reasons cited by Rakos. Ulman has suggested that the economic success of Cuba over the past four years, since the beginning of the "rectification" program, proves that socialism can work. Whether we agree with Ulman or with Rakos, who suggests that Cuba's success may be due to Soviet subsidies, I think we can agree that it is too soon to tell whether Cuba's success is real or illusory. (Author's note: this passage has been left as it was in the original paper. However, recent developments bear commenting upon. The rectification program is an attempt by Cuba to organize volunteer worker brigades to do the tasks Cuba needs done in order to function. By all accounts, the program is continuing and running well. However, the collapse of the Soviet Union and the removal of their subsidies has apparently led to widespread financial difficulties within Cuba. Where the country will now head is uncertain.)

The success of capitalism (and its weakness) is due to its competitive nature. Nothing is assured, and successful business and industry behavior are selected by their consequences. The savings and loan fiasco aside, such consequences as profits and continued existence generally select industry behavior. The problem inherent in this system was touched upon by Morrow (1988). He mentions that the distribution of available reinforcers under capitalism is positively skewed, to say the least. In a competitive situation there must always be winners and losers. The problem with pure capitalism is that losers lose big, and there are no resources for those who lose to fall back upon. This in turn has serious consequences for the nation as a whole (hence the New Deal of Roosevelt).

WELFARE

This last point is questioned by libertarians, who regard socialism as "envy writ large, and elevated to a moral ideal. It brands the most productive as criminals and makes heroes of those who have difficulty achieving anything at all" (Sheaffer 1989, p. 20). While it is tempting to write the whole matter off as "haves" who see no reason to give to the "have nots," there is a serious behavioral notion in question.

Among libertarians, there is a theory known as the "quick as hell" theory, which states that as soon as welfare and unemployment benefits are no longer available, everyone who doesn't have a job will find one, quick as hell. The obvious implication is that people who receive some sort of government relief are lazy or unmotivated, or, more charitably, have figured the system out. (Although perhaps this radical version of capitalist thinking is not widespread, the general idea is well-grounded in popular thought, hence the success of Ronald Reagan's "people on welfare driving cadillacs" rhetoric). Attributing behavior to something inherent in the individual is contrary to what behavior analysis has taught us about human conduct. If we must blame, we should blame the contingencies that have led to this "inactive" behavior (Holland 1978), including the welfare system itself, which punishes independent earning with lessened benefits.

To behaviorists, the crucial question of welfare comes down

to whether or not inactivity and increases in family size are re-inforced by welfare benefits. The answer is, of course, that in some cases it does and in other cases it does not. The truth is that most people on welfare do not become life-long recipients. It is my impression, formed from my work as a crime victims counselor in New York City's social services network, that most people on welfare do not particularly enjoy the experience and use welfare only as a temporary resource. On the other hand, to anyone who went through public school in any large city in the United States, it was no news to meet a third-generation welfare recipient or a teenage woman who had had a child so as to begin receiving welfare benefits as a separate family unit. It is the double-edged nature of the evidence that so confounds the question.

Pure capitalism and vacuum behaviorism would eliminate welfare because it's counter-productive for the recipient. It's a poor strategy to provide noncontingent reinforcement and expect be-havior to change only in desired directions. We are not living in a vacuum, however. In my work, for example, I often came across battered women who wished to leave their abusive husbands. Many had no financial resources for themselves or (usually) for their children. To eliminate welfare is to force such people to stay in the abusive situation, or to be thrown out on the street. Economic disasters are also faced by families in which the main provider becomes seriously ill, or in geographic areas where a large source of employment (e.g., a mill or factory) closes. For just such emer-gencies at least temporary welfare must be available. This is not only a humanitarian argument, it is a practical one as well. Without the means to obtain material reinforcers, crime becomes more probable (the counter-control that often follows aversive conditions [Sidman 1989]). Further, a country in which the population cannot afford the products of its industry will face economic hardship unless it has a large export over import surplus (which the United States does not).

As a provision of the federal Family Support Act of 1988, many states are now trying to eliminate the noncontingent nature of welfare, forcing recipients to accept jobs or education in return for their benefits ("workfare"). Setting aside arguments about whether or not some people should be given what other people have to work long hard hours to obtain, in February of 1990 the City University of New York announced a study demonstrating that welfare recipients who receive a college education leave the welfare rolls. Many other problems will become apparent and require attention as a result of this effort (e.g., child care must be made available, serious remedial education will be required before many are ready to take jobs, and the problem described by Rakos—you can make benefits contingent on showing up for work, but getting people to be productive is quite another matter). Nonetheless, living on welfare is not a particularly pleasant experience. Perhaps if the productive behavior of recipients is reinforced, the effects will generalize and self-help behavior will begin to be exhibited (as suggested by Miller and Miller 1970).

It is clear that neither pure capitalism nor pure socialism is likely to be helpful in the areas described above. Pure capitalism is preferable only if one is willing to accept a situation of "every person for her/himself" and the inevitable disaster that will result for a large segment of the population and possibly for the greater society as well. If this is not acceptable, then some "socialist" interventions are required. State control must be balanced along with exposure to naturally occurring contingencies. The state controls function to equalize the disparity between short-term reinforcers and long-term punishers. It is also hoped that they will prevent problems that can rise from the behavior of following short-term reinforcers.

To this end, behavior analysts may design any social policy. Of course, the problem of how to get the designed policy implemented still exists. The fact that a practice achieves stated goals provides no guarantee that it will be appreciated or implemented. Geller (1989) has described an integration of applied behavior analysis and social marketing with regard to popularizing behavioral interventions aimed at environmentally relevant behavior. His strategy involves appreciating the contingencies influencing, and designing interventions addressing, the various groups involved in the problem area (including government officials). His strategy lends itself to a systematic effort regarding the political process and may provide the route by which behavioral strategies will make their way into government policy.

We must, however, be willing to test the effectiveness of any proposed intervention and if need be reject established policy, even if this action conflicts with political ideology. It is not an easy step to take—witness the disastrous seventy-eight-year-old "drug war" (Marshall 1988)—but it is essential if we are to keep our status as behavior analysts rather than political ideologues. A Comte-inspired "behaviorist" political party would consist of individuals who had tired of the promises of political philosophy and who instead trust empiricism as the path to designing policy. As Rakos (1988b) himself says, "we must employ scientific analyses rather than political ones, since in the long run, a more equitable and just society will depend more on empiricism than on ideology." I would add that the empiricism must be more problem-specific than Rakos's general approach.

It might be suggested that this would be impossible and that as soon as behavior analysts move into the social environment they go beyond the data and lose the behaviorally structured, nonideological stance. I would disagree and cite the Los Horcones (1989) community as evidence. Policies there are attempted and, if they do not achieve their desired aims, they are changed. The behavior analysts at Los Horcones are not going beyond their data. Instead, the data are derived from the policies they design. The behavior analysts are active members of the community, but can, because of their emphasis on empiricism, remain free of any other political ideology. This is the framework from which I make my suggestion of a nonideological stance. The conclusions I drew as to what type of policies in each problem area would be required are tentative and open to test. If they proved to be ineffective or damaging, then they would be changed.

It should come as no surprise that no single political policy or philosophy that attempts to cross all areas can supply all the answers. We would never seriously suggest that all problems can be solved by the institution of a single procedure (e.g., "overcorrection will solve all behavior problems"). By the same token, we should not suggest that any one political philosophy is likely to provide all the answers. Only by examining each problem area as its own subject matter will we be able to make a serious contribution to the design of public policy.

THE DRUG CRISIS:
A DESCRIPTION OF CONTINGENCIES

In the summer of 1989, George Bush proposed a multi-billion dollar plan to combat the "drug crisis" faced by the United States. His plan follows the pattern set by Ronald Reagan's "war on drugs," and attempts to eliminate drug use and trade. Also during the summer of 1989, the Libertarian party called for the legalization of illegal drugs in order to alleviate that same crisis. Few problems are considered more pressing in the United States, and strong feelings have been expressed from all ends of the political spectrum regarding strategy for the war on drugs (e.g., Marshall 1988a, Muck 1988).

The "drug crisis" is a summary term given for a cluster of behavior that surrounds the trade and use of currently illegal drugs. There are two aspects to the drug crisis: the individual and the societal. On the individual level there is the physical addiction and subsequent disruption of life associated with drug dependency (American Psychiatric Association 1987), as well as the lifestyle created by drug legislation (Brecher et al. 1972). On the societal level there is the phenomenon of the "drug turf" (and subsequent violent "turf wars," which increasingly imprison our citizens in their homes and lead to the deaths of innocents), the danger posed to others by the addicted individual both through crime and impaired functioning, the overloading of our courts and prisons, the threat of political corruption, the tremendous drain of resources in attempting to enforce drug laws, and the adverse effects in drug-growing countries caused by the power of "drug lords" (Marshall 1988a).

Contingencies for the Individual Drug User

The behavior of the drug user and the presumed consequences of this behavior are at the very core of the drug debate. It is, supposedly, the danger to the addicted individual and others who come into contact with him/her that is behind the whole drug uproar. There is also the matter of moral absolutism. As pointed out by Szasz (1990), the drug uproar closely mirrors other issues in which the Judeo-Christian ethic against giving in to pleasurable temptation has been central. These arguments will be addressed in a subsequent section regarding contingencies influencing policy makers. The drug user is seen as unpredictable and dangerous, and it is feared that the person will introduce others to drugs ("contagion"—e.g., the scare film *Reefer Madness;* laughable to today's mainstream society in its sensationalism and misinformation, the government's rhetoric regarding drug policy has changed little since the film's debut). When attempting to describe the contingencies that influence the behavior of the drug user, however, it is important to keep in mind the distinction between contingencies created by drug intake and contingencies created by drug legislation. Brecher et al. (1972), for example, have conducted a historical and cross-cultural study of the use and trade of currently illegal drugs. They have made a very strong case that the problems we commonly attribute to drug intake are actually a result of the lifestyle the drug user is forced into by current drug legislation. In order to properly assess the effects of these two different sets of contingencies, it is necessary to examine historical and cross-cultural research in addition to the more traditional research discussed below. Unfortunately, much of the research regarding the drug crisis is of an unreliable survey nature (Michaels 1987), with the distinction between drug use-created and drug law-created contingencies badly underappreciated. Misinformation regarding the effects of drug use and the results of international drug policy is also widespread (Brecher et al. 1972) and disseminated in accord with political goals (Michaels 1987); we must therefore be careful when evaluating "evidence." There are several conclusions, however, that we can confidently draw regarding the effects of drug use and drug laws.

Several processes play a role in the genesis and maintenance of individual drug usage. The initiation of drug use has been attributed to modeling effects (Kandel 1978) and also to negative reinforcement from peer pressure (Fulmer and Lapidus 1980). The reinforcement paradigm, as described by Herrnstein's hyperbola (1970), must also be appreciated (R. F. Rakos, personal communication, November 28, 1989).

Herrnstein's hyperbola is a mathematical equation that describes the progression of reinforcement effects and suggests that reinforcers must be considered relative to all other reinforcers in the environment in order to predict effects (McDowell 1982). Given this latter assertion, we can better conceptualize the behavior of drug use, particularly in economically depressed inner-city areas. In areas devastated by, among other things, the last ten years of federal policies toward the poor, the range of available reinforcers is severely limited. The powerful effects of drugs thus stand out against a backdrop of poverty and hopelessness (particularly when an individual lacks marketable skills) as an attainable and immediate source of reinforcement (i.e., pleasurable physical effects, a sense of self-efficacy or purpose, temporary escape from despair, etc.). To prevent drug use, then, it is imperative that other reinforcers be readily available to the potential user. Unfortunately, they often are not. From this perspective, policies such as "just say no" seem like cruel irony: first the government withdraws sources of reinforcement (e.g., financial aid for education, job training, social services, and the like) and then it moralistically tells people to avoid remaining sources of reinforcement. Such an approach blames the victim (Ryan 1970), ignores the social contingencies that created the problem (e.g., Holland 1978), and, furthermore, presumes that self-control is simply a matter of willpower. However, self-control research suggests that the immediate reinforcers maintaining drug use will prove difficult to resist: organisms prefer immediate reinforcers to delayed reinforcers, even if the latter are twice as large as the former (Rachlin and Green 1972).

Once the behavior is established, the most obvious reinforcer maintaining drug intake is, of course, the drug itself (McAuliffe and Gordon 1980). Currently illegal drugs, many of which have been used across cultures for centuries, produce powerful physical effects and often addiction (or, in the old tongue, dangerous moral weakness). This perceived danger, along with assorted political and racist reasons, is why many drugs were declared illegal in the first place (Hamowy 1987, Musto 1987). Addicted lab animals will perform grueling tasks for a "fix" (Woods 1978). Likewise, addicted humans will do whatever is necessary to obtain their drugs. Many addicts have reported total life disruption as their drug became their all-consuming reinforcer (Sutker and Archer 1984), although this phenomenon may be more a function of contingencies created by drug legislation than drug use per se.

As opposed to the drug intake-created contingencies described above, drug legislation has created several contingencies that must be appreciated in order to understand the individual level of the drug crisis. Our stereotypical picture of the drug user is that of the "junkie," an individual who gives up all resources for drugs and whose body is slowly falling apart. This picture, however, is more accurately assigned to the influence of drug laws than drug use itself. Statutes prohibiting drug use have created a contingency such that being caught using or trading drugs often leads to being imprisoned or fined. Although we will see that these punishers are ineffective in halting drug trade and use, this contingency has forced users into behavior that would be unnecessary in the absence of the drug law. Such laws drive up the price of drugs, thereby prompting the user to commit crimes and forego food and medical care, force the user to spend time attempting to buy drugs rather than engaging in more constructive behavior, force the user to buy drugs that may be impure, and encourage the user to abandon mainstream society and join the drug subculture. Most importantly, it is the drug laws and the media's attention to them (which glamorizes drug use and makes it seem illicit and therefore thrilling) and not the behavior of any individual user that lead to huge rises in the social level of drug use (Brecher et al. 1972, Zinberg 1987). Drug users are not somehow lacking in morality; their behavior follows the same laws that govern any other operant response.

To test the hypothesis that drug laws and not the drugs themselves are the cause of supposed "anti-social" behavior, we must question whether this behavior was present in the addict population before the drug laws were enacted or in places where the laws were never enacted. While the physical effects of the drugs certainly preceded the drug laws, the anti-social behavior did not; nor, with the possible exception of "speed," historically or cross-culturally, was anti-social behavior spontaneously emitted in places where a supply of drugs was not limited by legislation or politics (Brecher et al. 1972). Even in the case of speed, limiting access and criminalizing use and trade did little more than popularize the drug (a familiar trend in drug legislation). The addicted individual may introduce others to the drug, but it is the drug laws and media attention that have historically led to huge increases in the social level of use of any given drug. The addict is thus probably an "expert" who is consulted once interest has been roused.

Given that drugs do not in and of themselves lead to anti-social activities, drug laws can only be justified from a moralistic standpoint or in terms of a paternal desire to "protect the user from him/herself." While such protection might be a noble ambition (though based on faulty knowledge of the effects of drug use), it (a) is misdirected and useless in the absence of changes in the conditions that lead to drug use in the first place, and (b) paradoxically achieves the opposite effect, i.e., popularizing drug use. Further, temporally distant, intermittently produced, and low-intensity punishers are relatively impotent compared with immediate positive reinforcers (Skinner 1989). Against immediate reinforcers of drug usage, society's application of temporally distant, contrived punishers such as imprisonment or fines have been virtually useless (Hamowy 1987, Whitlock 1987). Drug use is in all probability here to stay, and drug laws only exacerbate the situation.

Contingencies for the Drug Trader

Drug use is initiated and maintained by social conditions and by the addictive qualities of the drugs themselves. Drug trading, however, is created and maintained by the contingencies of drug legislation. Cooper, Heron, and Heward (1987) describe "setting events," stimulus-response interactions that alter stimulus-response interactions that follow. Extending this concept to our current discussion, legislation limiting drug use and trade is a stimulus that has strengthened the drug use lifestyle described above by creating a tremendous black market for currently illegal drugs. Drug prices are inflated several hundred percent on this black market, making trade in illegal drugs extremely profitable (Barnett 1987). It is this profit factor that leads to violent turf wars as rival gangs battle for territories in which to conduct their business. When drugs are available legally, there is little need for a black market and prices are maintained at a tolerable level. When the drug supply falls into the hands of the black marketeers, however, the addict has no choice but to pay exorbitant prices. Like other businesspeople enjoying a large profit margin, black marketeers try to expand their operation. This expansion exacerbates the problems we currently experience. Drug laws thus bring about the very conditions they are intended to prevent.

As with the user's/behavior, society's contrived punishers are virtually useless in effecting behavior change in drug traders. Herrnstein's hyperbola predicts this outcome, particularly in economically depressed areas where individuals often lack marketable skills and where drug trade may thus appear as the only route to the social reinforcers of financial security. Besides, it is usually only a user or minor courier who is caught and brought up on charges. The real sources (the drug kingpins) are rarely apprehended, and for every minor player who is taken out of the game, there is a substitute eager to fill the vacancy.

One of the great virtues of behavior analysis is its emphasis upon evaluating the results of interventions rather than relying on preconceived notions. Our current drug situation can be likened to an example from the clinical literature regarding how best to handle a misbehaving child. In the case of the child, attention (reinforcement) is attained for the misbehavior. The unacceptable behavior will persist as long as it is reinforced with attention. Historically, the same effect has occurred with drug legislation. While the intentions of righteous attention are noble, the behavioral effects run counter to the purpose of the legislation. Conceptualizing the question from a research standpoint, the "A" of our AB design would be pre-1914 (Harrison Narcotics Act implemented). We can think of 1914 as the point at which the "B" phase begins. The B phase has seen an exacerbation of the problems we sought to solve. For the past seventy-eight years we have poured more and more resources into efforts to eliminate drug trade and use without ever bothering to note what the results of these efforts are (Barnett 1987, Marshall 1988c). An appreciation of the behavioral effects of drug laws is seriously overdue. Either a return to baseline or a "C" phase (possibly of regulated legalization) is clearly indicated.

Contingencies for Policy Makers

The relevant behavior of policy makers includes the introduction and enforcement of drug laws, as well as using their influence to make "the drug crisis" a pressing issue. Responses that have produced reinforcing consequences are maintained in the behavioral repertoire. Clearly, attempts at drug law enforcement have been dismal failures and have led to great damage. There would thus seem to be a contradiction here. The fact that drug laws have continued to be enforced and made more and more severe, despite the damage they have done, suggests that something other than a desire to protect public interest is involved (which we could also infer from the behavior of U.S. Commissioner of Narcotics Harry Anslinger, an adamant anti-drug influence who nonetheless provided a steady supply of narcotics to an addicted member of Congress, as reported by Brecher et al. [1972, pp. 36-37]). We must conclude that there is something beyond the stated intentions of drug legislation that leads policy makers to continue this damaging battle. Therefore, the task before us is to identify the reinforcing elements in current drug policy.

Listening to the Reagan/Bush rhetoric, it might be supposed that moralizing and shrewd politics are at the root of the drug hysteria. This idea has some historical support, including the spearheading efforts of William Jennings Bryan (the famed fundamentalist prosecutor from the Scopes trial) regarding the legislation that would set the pattern for drug laws in the United States, the Harrison Narcotics Act of 1914. It is possible that the Protestant ethic, which provides little sympathy for "deviants" such as drug addicts, plays a role in the ongoing battle against drugs. This would also explain the rhetoric against methadone maintenance, namely, that it is simply exchanging one crutch for another. Drug use, according to this line of thought, should be stopped by force of will ("just say no"). The popularity of the Protestant ethic (a "rule" that changes little, if at all, with the actual contingencies) in the United States makes for very easy scapegoating of the addict (Szasz 1987); or, if any sympathy is evoked for the drug user, it is rapidly changed into violent anger against the "pusher," who has replaced the "Communist" as the great faceless threat to American values (Singer, quoted in Marshall 1987). This makes a very efficient distraction and allows the policy maker to avoid addressing the social conditions that created the drug use originally. Certainly, none of the history we have examined should be news to President Bush, and yet his rhetoric on the "drug crisis" consists largely of moralizing, while he remains completely oblivious of the historical facts regarding efforts to eliminate drugs. To go beyond our data, then, these moralistic and political ideas may, unfortunately be more accurate than we would idealistically like to believe of our president (who we hope would have the well-being of the country, rather than ideology or political popularity, at heart). Perhaps even more distressing, however, are charges that the "drug crisis" is really a cover that allows the federal government to carry out unpopular foreign policy (Marshall 1987), including the support of brutal and oppressive governments.

Let us ignore these possible motivators, however, and examine the contingencies faced by the government official. Given the assumption that those in government have come to the conclusion that drug legalization is the proper course of action, what would be the contingencies facing these officials? Government officials are under serious contingencies; the unpopularity of certain stances, e.g., drug legalization, which makes the punisher of losing an election or being voted out of office a virtual certainty if the candidate appears to hold the unpopular view (Skinner 1989). With only a few notable exceptions, politicians who advocate drug legalization never make it into office, or, if they do, they soon leave. In contrast, being "tough on drugs" has proven to be a winning strategy. This stance is thus maintained by the powerful reinforcers of power and influence.

The Bush Plan: Educate, Treat, Enforce

In the tradition of Bryan, Anslinger, and the Harrison Narcotics Act, the Bush drug initiative follows the "educate, treat, eliminate, and punish" approach advocated by Ronald Reagan. Against the powerful contingencies governing drug use and trade, however, Reagan's strategy was ineffective, to put it mildly (Marshall 1988c). For all the billions Bush has set aside for preventive education, treatment, elimination, and punishment, his plan does not address the contingencies of drug use and trade, the conditions that created the drug use, nor the side-effects of attempting to stop consumption and trade. Historically, such efforts have been dismal failures and have exacerbated the very problems they sought to solve. Assuming that solving the problems caused by drug use (which are more accurately conceptualized as due to drug laws) is the actual goal, the Bush effort is clearly misdirected.

The large numbers of high school and college-age drug users (Barnes 1988) challenge the efficacy of past efforts at preventive education. Some researchers have gone so far as to call these efforts a failure (e.g., Zinberg 1987). This can be explained in several ways. First, the main assumption of the education approach— if people were aware of the effects of drug use then they would not take drugs—is probably faulty. Although many users did not believe they would get addicted, to suggest that new drug users have no knowledge of the possible adverse consequences of their actions and choices is unreasonable. Second, the education effort has been mishandled. Drug education has consisted of sensationalized misinformation and warnings (Hamowy 1987, Zinberg 1987), and it has been suggested (Brecher et al. 1972) that the failure of education efforts may be due to the fact that young users see that they have been fed lies. They then assume that nothing they have been told about the harmful effects of drugs can be true. Third, the education approach completely misses the point raised earlier about the scarcity of alternate reinforcers available in the addict's environment and the skill deficits of the users that often are evident as well. Fourth and finally, some behavior produces such potent reinforcement that knowledge of the inherent dangers is an insufficient deterrent. Even given the negative effects of drug use under current drug laws, the reinforcers that are provided by drug use and trade (e.g., the physical high and the financial rewards) are too powerful to be countered by the known dangers (a point that we could also extend to nicotine, alcohol, sugar, salt, and caffeine consumption). As might be expected, the success rates of treatments aimed at breaking drug addiction are poor (Burt, Brown, and DuPont 1980; Meyer and Salmon 1984).

Drug traffic would in all probability not be significantly hampered by increased border patrols. Even as highly regulated a "society" as the U.S. Army has been unable to stop drug traffic among its members (Brecher et al. 1972). The United States is too large and there are too many ways to get drugs into the country (Marshall 1988b); thus, despite all the resources already spent on attempts to keep drugs out of the country, virtually anyone who wants drugs can get them easily (Michaels 1987). Even if it were more successful than the Reagan plan, the Bush proposal would lead to increased violence as a lessened supply of drugs would increase their already inflated price and thus force addicts to perpetrate even more crimes in order to support their addictions.

Or, less drastically, drug users would simply change their drug of choice (Brecher et al. 1972). The "elimination" attempt, although perhaps born of noble intentions, would in all probability be a waste of time, money, and lives.

Additionally, as we have seen, drugs are too powerful a reinforcer for our temporally distant, intermittently applied, low-intensity contrived punishers to alter the behavior of users and especially traders. Historically, even punishments that would be considered barbaric by our standards have been ineffective in limiting drug use and trade (Brecher et al. 1972). This pattern is currently being repeated in several countries throughout the world. Despite claims to the contrary, severe penalties, including the death penalty without benefit of a trial, have been ineffective in limiting drug use and trade (Michaels 1987, Trebach 1987). The call for more severe penalties thus makes for nice political rhetoric but for poor strategy. The Bush initiative would alleviate neither the individual nor the societal aspects of the drug crisis, and would probably exacerbate both.

THE LEGALIZATION ALTERNATIVE

Proponents of legalization, on the other hand, suggest that attempting to eliminate drug use and trade is futile. Rather than attempt eradication, they seek to regulate the use and sale of drugs. (They have read their sociology: they know that socially labeled deviance cannot be eliminated, but only regulated.) There are many views on how this regulation would be accomplished, but one option is to treat currently illegal drugs like currently legal drugs (such as tobacco and alcohol) and allow a semi-free market. While this might be acceptable for a drug such as marijuana, the policy would probably not be viable for the more powerful drugs. Regulating sales would be difficult, and large corporations and their advertising firms are probably not the ones we should count on to suggest responsible usage. Their own contingencies force them to drive sales up to as high a level as possible, and that is not the goal of any responsible drug policy. Another option is to place the burden for dispensing drugs in the hands of the medical profession and specialized dispensing centers. This latter option is particularly attractive because it embraces a more realistic view of drug treatment. Due to the reinforcing properties of drugs, total abstinence may be an impossible goal for most. The poor success rates of treatment centers testifies to this possibility. Perhaps maintenance at the lowest possible levels would be a more achievable goal. The fact that many users do not become addicts suggests that controlled usage should be seriously explored as an option (Zinberg 1987), as it has been with nicotine (e.g., Glasgow, Morray, and Lichtenstein 1989) and alcohol (e.g., Sobell and Sobell 1984). Regardless of the exact path chosen, the legalization initiative would also have both individual and societal side-effects.

Most seriously, drug usage would probably increase. An argument could be made that this would not occur, given that the established contingencies have been demonstrated ineffective at halting drug usage and trade and that virtually anyone who wants drugs can get them. However, using prohibition as a historical precedent, we could predict a rise in the sheer number of users (Burnham and Kerr 1988). In reality, we would have to be willing to accept the probability of a percentage of the population being perpetually addicted to currently illegal drugs (given an assumption of no change in the economic and social conditions that give rise to drug use in the first place). We must, however, keep in mind that this is what we face currently, and there are no indications that this will change. Furthermore, society tolerates addiction to nicotine (and the one thousand people who die each day from cigarettes in the United States [Goldstein and Krasner 1987]) as well as alcohol (Barnes 1988). Another negative side-effect of legalization would be the probable need for widespread drug testing in professions and areas where public safety is at stake (although arguments have been made that this is already necessary [see Stone and Thompson 1989]). Other side-effects would be more positive: a drop in crime as the price of drugs drop several hundred percent, a great increase in the quality of living for the addict, relief for our overburdened legal and corrections systems, enormous revenue from legal drug trade instead of billions spent on enforcement (profit that could be put toward research on treatment and education, which might increase their efficacy, as well as toward ending the social conditions that give rise to the drug use), the end of the American drug turf war, and the end of the drug lords. There would seem to be no problem legalization would bring about that we do not already see in abundance. Legalization might increase the sheer number of users, but it would certainly improve the lot of the user and would alleviate many problems of the social level of the drug crisis.

Clearly, there are serious issues to consider before changing drug policy. Nonetheless, an analysis of contingencies suggests that legalization will lead to the greater good. What must be acknowledged is that without efforts to improve the social conditions that lead to drug use in the first place, efforts to eliminate drug consumption and trafficking are pointless. The contingencies that support drug use and trade are too powerful. Given that no changes occur in the social conditions that give rise to drug use, we will always have a percentage of the population addicted to illegal drugs. An analysis of history and relevant contingencies suggests that President Bush's policy will continue to be ineffective; it suggests legalization as the strategy that will alleviate many of the societal and individual aspects of the drug crisis. The war on drugs is a losing battle, one that should have never begun.

As stated earlier, government officials are under strict contingencies regarding the drug crisis. Any indication of being "soft on drugs" is an invitation to be voted out of office. A social marketing strategy for legalization is thus required in order to alter voting patterns and consequently shape the behavior of legislators. Prohibition was not ended because of its adverse effects; it was ended because "the propaganda war" was won by those in favor of legalization (Burnham and Kerr 1988). Obviously, the adverse effects of criminalizing drug usage and trade have not been enough to change the behavior of legislators either.

Other groups, e.g., the Libertarian and Humanist groups, share the legalization conclusion. Social marketing efforts could be done in association with such organizations. The drug crisis will not go away by throwing more and more resources at programs that have been shown to be ineffective and damaging. With each new effort to "crack down," the drug crisis only gets worse. Social marketing aimed at the government and the media will have to be undertaken so as to allow the legalization process to begin. This will be the first step in alleviating a large part of the drug crisis and it will have to begin soon. "Ice," a smokable amphetamine derivative with powerful and comparatively long-lasting effects, has made its debut in our streets. Given the potential profits of trade in this increasingly popular drug, wars between drug trading gangs will be bloodier than ever. We need to evaluate our drug policy and to realize that it is not achieving its stated aims. Not only is it not reducing the problem, current drug policy is actually exacerbating it. Anti-cigarette smoking campaigns have been successfully conducted without the horrible side-effects of making the drug illegal (e.g., Pierce, Macaskill, Mappstat, and Hill [1990]). It is time for those leading the war on drugs to learn from this example.

IS SOCIAL PLANNING DEHUMANIZING?

It has long been discussed in utopian and dystopian literature (see Newman 1992) that such an emphasis on the analysis of empirical data in the area of social planning may lead to the loss of some of the elements of life we hold most dear (e.g., freedom, challenges to overcome, "the right to be unhappy"). Many such works have warned us that efforts to apply the scientific method to public policy will lead to a most unhumanistic social arrangement, one in which our very humanity will be lost and heartless "data" will be our master rather than our servant.

Many such novels have an emotional appeal that can make social planning efforts seem quite undesirable. If we avoid social planning and allow public policy to be dictated by something other than empirical data, however, are we truly encouraging a humanistic outlook? Or, are we sowing the seeds that will lead to our own dehumanization?

Looking back to chapter 1, we must remind ourselves of Lamont's notion that the Humanist advocates bold applications of the scientific method to the problems confronting society. To echo Skinner once more, there is no virtue in accident. The use of science in the design of public policy is in the best tradition of humanistic thought, and we should embrace such behavioral science with zeal. With no less zeal, however, we must analyze to what ends this science should be applied.

Epilogue

It should be apparent from the preceding chapters that behavioral forces are at work, whether we consciously design them or not. They are inherent at every level of social interaction and are at work throughout society. Behavior is selected by its consequences, just as surely as genetic variations are. Ignoring this fact will not be helpful. What will be helpful is to acknowledge this fact, however unpleasant it may occasionally be, and to take advantage of it. Behavior analysis is in the best tradition of the humanist philosophy. We should do as the humanist philosophy suggests and use the findings of science and reason to achieve the goal of human fulfillment in this world. Since the fall of the medieval world-view, the humanist philosophy has taught us that the good for humans in this world should be the paramount concern of any social system. Behavior analysis, applied in keeping with humanist philosophy, can help us to act effectively on this concern.

We have looked at various areas where humanism and behavior analysis have been considered polar opposites. I hope that I have been able to demonstrate that this is not a necessary conclusion and is, in fact, incorrect. In view of the current analysis, the old hostilities between the two systems are quite inappropriate. Championing one system and denigrating the other simply shows an incompleteness of thought. Humanists who detract from behavior analysis (perhaps because of arguments we have challenged) show that they are actively avoiding considering a large body of experimental research. This is, of course, quite in contrast to their stated dedication to the scientific method. Behavior analysts who wish to detract from the humanist system and deny its usefulness may do so. If they do, however, they must also be prepared to admit that the behavioral system possesses no means of guiding applications and be prepared to suggest an alternate guiding philosophy. I have tried to make a case that the humanistic system is in keeping with the history, philosophy, and practice of behavior analysis and is therefore an appropriate philosophy for this task.

B. F. Skinner, of course, presupposed this conclusion. He served as a member of the editorial board of *The Humanist* for many years, and, as mentioned, was named "Humanist of the Year"' for 1972. He seemed to think it self-evident that the two systems have much to offer one another, an argument that I hope has been supported here.

References

Agras, W. S., R. G. Jacob, and M. Lebedeck. 1980. "The California Drought: A Quasi-Experimental Analysis of Social Policy." *Journal of Applied Behavior Analysis* 13: 561–70.

Aiken, H. D. 1956. *The Age of Ideology*. New York: The New American Library.

American Psychiatric Association. 1987. *Diagnostic and Statistical Manual of Mental Disorders* (3d ed. revised). Washington, D.C.

Bacon-Prue, A., R. Blount, D. Pickering, and R. Drabman. 1980. "An Evaluation of Three Litter Control Procedures—Trash Receptacles, Paid Workers, and the Marked Item Technique." *Journal of Applied Behavior Analysis* 13: 165–70.

Baer, D. M. 1989. "A Behavior-Analytic Account of Human Development." Paper presented at the 1989 meeting of the Society for Research in Child Development, Kansas City, Missouri.

Bandura, A. 1986. *Social Foundations of Thought and Action: A Social Cognitive Theory*. Englewood Cliffs, N.J.: Prentice-Hall, Inc.

Barnes, D. M. 1988. "Drugs: Running the Numbers." *Science* 240, 1729–31.

Barnett, R. E. 1987. "Curing the Drug-law Addiction: The Harmful

Side Effects of Legal Prohibition." In *Dealing with Drugs,* R. Hamowy, ed. Toronto: Lexington Books, 73–102.

Bettelheim, B. 1987. "Discussion of Therapy in Our Day." In *The Evolution of Psychotherapy,* J. K. Zeig, ed. New York: Brunner/Mazel Inc., 219–20.

Bijou, S. W. 1970. "What Psychology Has to Offer Education—Now." *Journal of Applied Behavior Analysis* 3: 65–71.

Binder, C., and C. L. Watkins. 1989. "Promoting Effective Instructional Methods: Solutions to America's Educational Crisis." *Future Choices* 1(3): 33-39.

Brecher, E. M., and the editors of *Consumer Reports.* (1972). *Licit and Illicit Drugs.* Boston: Little, Brown, and Company.

Brinckerhoff, R. 1971. "Freudianism, Behaviorism, and Humanism." *The Humanist* 31(2): 16-17.

Broden, M., R. V. Hall, and B. Mitts. 1971. "The Effect of Self-recording on the Classroom Behavior of Two Eighth-grade Students." *Journal of Applied Behavior Analysis* 4: 191–99.

Bruckner-Gordon, F., B. K. Gangi, and G. U. Wallman. 1988. *Making Therapy Work.* New York: Harper and Row.

Burgess, A. 1986. *A Clockwork Orange.* New York: Ballantine Books.

Burnham, J. C. and K. A. Kerr. 1988. "The Lessons of Prohibition." *USA Today* (Newsletter section) 117(2523): 6.

Burt, M. R., B. S. Brown, and R. L. DuPont. 1980. "Follow-up of Former Clients of a Large Multimodality Drug Treatment Program." *International Journal of the Addictions* 15: 391–408.

Butterfield, H. 1957. *The Origins of Modern Science.* New York: The Free Press.

Carnine, D. 1988. "Breaking the Failure Cycle in the Elementary School." *Youth Policy* 10(7): 22–25.

Carpenter, F. 1974. *The Skinner Primer: Behind Freedom and Dignity.* New York: The Free Press.

Catania, C. 1975. "The Myth of Self-reinforcement." *Behaviorism* 3: 192–99.

———. 1984. *Learning,* 2d ed. Englewood Cliffs, N.J.: Prentice-Hall.

Caufield, C. 1984. *In the Rainforest.* Chicago: The University of Chicago Press.

Cohen, H. L., and J. Filipczak. 1989. *A New Learning Environment*. Boston: Authors Cooperative.

Cone, J. D., and S. C. Hayes. 1984. *Environmental Problems: Behavioral Solutions*. New York: Cambridge University Press.

Cook, D. A. 1988. "Educational Technology and Opportunity." *Youth Policy* 10(7): 2–3.

Cooper, J. O., T. E. Heron, and W. L. Heward. 1987. *Applied Behavior Analysis*. Toronto, Canada: Merrill Publishing.

Corsini, R. J. 1984. *Current Psychotherapies,* 3d ed. Itasca, Ill.: F. E. Peacock Publishing.

Cossairt, A., R. V. Hall, and B. L. Hopkins. 1973. "The Effects of Experimenter's Instructions, Feedback, and Praise on Teacher Praise and Student Attending Behavior." *Journal of Applied Behavior Analysis* 6: 89–100.

Day, W. F. 1971. "Humanistic Psychology and Contemporary Behaviorism." *The Humanist* 31(2): 13–17.

Deluty, M. Z. 1978. "Self-control and Impulsiveness Involving Aversive Events." *Journal of Experimental Psychology: Animal Behavior Processes* 4: 250–66.

Diamond, J. 1989. "Publish or Perish." *Discover* 10(7): 96–101.

Dickinson, A. M. 1989. "The Detrimental Effects of Extrinsic Reinforcement on 'Intrinsic Motivation.' " *The Behavior Analyst* 12: 1–15.

Dorow, L. G. 1988. "Educating Our Youth: Proposals for Reform." *Youth Policy* 10(7): 31–32.

Drabman, R. S., and B. B. Lahey. 1974. "Feedback in Classroom Behavior Modification: Effects on the Target and Her Classmates." *Journal of Applied Behavior Analysis* 7: 591–98.

Duke, C., S. Fried, W. Piley, and D. Walker. 1989. "Contributions to the History of Psychology: LIX. Rosalie Rayner Watson: The Mother of a Behaviorist's Sons." *Psychological Reports* 65: 163–69.

Ehrenberg, O., and M. Ehrenberg. 1986. *The Psychotherapy Maze*. New York: Simon and Schuster.

Fawcett, S. B., R. M. Mathews, and R. K. Fletcher. 1980. "Some Promising Dimensions for Behavioral Community Technology." *Journal of Applied Behavior Analysis* 13: 505–18.

Fornos, W. 1987. *Gaining People, Losing Ground: A Blueprint for Stabilizing World Population*. Ephrata, Penn.: Science Press.

Fornos, W. 1990. "Gaining People, Losing Ground." *The Humanist* 50(3): 5–6.

Forsyth, A., and K. Miyata. 1984. *Tropical Nature.* New York: Charles Scribner's Sons.

Frost, S. E. 1942. *Basic Teachings of the Great Philosophers.* New York: Dolphin Books.

Fulmer, R. H., and L. B. Lapidus. 1980. "A Study of Professed Reasons for Beginning and Continuing Heroin Use." *International Journal of the Addictions* 15: 631–45.

Gardner, M. 1957. *Fads and Fallacies in the Name of Science.* New York: Dover Publications.

Geller, E. S. 1987. "Applied Behavior Analysis and Environmental Psychology: From Strange Bedfellows to a Productive Marriage." In *Handbook of Environmental Psychology,* D. Stokolos and I. Altman, eds., Vol. I. New York: John Wiley and Sons, 361–88.

————. 1989. "Applied Behavior Analysis and Social Marketing: An Integration for Environmental Preservation." *Journal of Social Issues* 45(1): 17–36.

Giles, T. R. 1983. "Probable Superiority of Behavioral Interventions–I: Traditional Comparative Outcome." *Journal of Behavior Therapy and Experimental Psychiatry* 14: 29–32.

————. 1990. "Bias Against Behavior Therapy in Outcome Reviews: Who Speaks for the Patient?" *The Behavior Therapist* 13: 86–90.

Glasgow, R. E., K. Morray, and E. Lichtenstein. 1989. "Controlled Smoking versus Abstinence as a Treatment Goal: The Hopes and Fears May be Unfounded." *Behavior Therapy* 20: 77–91.

Goetz, E. M., and D. M. Baer. 1973. "Social Control of Form Diversity and the Emergence of New Forms in Children's Blockbuilding." *Journal of Applied Behavior Analysis* 6: 209–17.

Goldiamond, I. 1976. "Self-reinforcement." *Journal of Applied Behavior Analysis* 9: 509–14.

Goldstein, A. P., and L. Krasner. 1987. *Modern Applied Psychology.* New York: Pergamon Press.

Goldstein, R. S., B. L. Minkin, N. Minkin, and D. M. Baer. 1978. "Finders Keepers?: An Analysis and Validation of a Free-found-ad Policy." *Journal of Applied Behavior Analysis* 11: 465–73.

Gould, S. J. 1981. *The Mismeasure of Man.* New York: W. W. Norton.

———. 1988. "Thoughts are Cheap." *The Skeptical Inquirer* 12(3): 243.

Gray, T. 1984. "University Course Reduces Belief in Paranormal." *The Skeptical Inquirer* 8(3): 247–51.

Greene, B. F., R. A. Winett, R. Van Houten, E. S. Geller, and B. A. Iwata. 1987. *Behavior Analysis in the Community.* Lawrence, Kansas: Society for the Experimental Analysis of Behavior, Inc.

Gross, M. 1986/1978. "The Psychological Society." In *Taking Sides: Clashing Views on Controversial Psychological Issues,* J. Rubinstein and B. Slife, eds. Guilford, Conn: The Dushkin Publishing Group, 313–22.

Guthrie, W. K. C. 1986. *Plato: Protagoras and Meno.* New York: Penguin Books.

Hamowy, R. 1987. *Dealing with Drugs.* Toronto: Lexington Books.

Hart, B. M., N. J. Reynolds, D. M. Baer, E. R. Brawley, and F. R. Harris. 1968. "Effect of Contingent and Noncontingent Social Reinforcement on the Cooperative Play of a Preschool Child." *Journal of Applied Behavior Analysis* 1: 73–76.

Harris, K. R. 1986. "Self-monitoring of Attentional Behavior versus Self-monitoring of Productivity: Effects of On-task Behavior and Academic Response Rate Among Learning Disabled Children." *Journal of Applied Behavior Analysis* 19: 417–24.

Hauserman, N., S. Walen, and M. Behling. 1973. "Reinforced Racial Integration in the First Grade: A Study in Generalization." *Journal of Applied Behavior Analysis* 6: 193–200.

Hawkins, R. P. 1985. "On Woolfolk and Richardson." *American Psychologist* 11: 1138–39.

Hearst, E. 1988. "Learning and Cognition." In *Stevens' Handbook of Experimental Psychology,* R. C. Atkinson, R. J. Herrnstein, G. Lindzey, and D. Luce, eds. New York: John Wiley and Sons, 1–109.

Holland, J. G. 1978. "Behaviorism: Part of the Problem or Part of the Solution?" *Journal of Applied Behavior Analysis* 11: 163–74.

Horney, K. 1942. *Self Analysis.* New York: W. W. Norton.

———. 1950. *Neurosis and Human Growth.* New York: W. W. Norton.

Huxley, A. 1958. *Brave New World Revisited.* New York: Harper and Row.

Kandel, D. B. 1978. "Convergences in Prospective Longitudinal Surveys of Drug Use in Normal Populations." In *Longitudinal Research on Drug Use: Empirical Findings and Methodological Issues,* D. B. Kandel, ed. Washington, D.C.: Hemisphere Publishing, 1–38.

Kazdin, A. E. 1982. *Single-case Research Designs.* New York: Oxford University Press.

Kendler, H. H. 1981. *Psychology: A Science in Conflict.* New York: Oxford University Press.

———. 1987. *Historical Foundations of Modern Psychology.* Chicago: The Dorsey Press.

Kneedler, R. D., and D. P. Hallahan. 1981. "Self-monitoring of On-task Behavior with Learning Disabled Children: Current Studies and Directions." *Exceptional Education Quarterly* 2(3): 73–82.

Koegel, R. L., and L. K. Koegel. 1990. "Extended Reductions in Stereotypic Behavior of Students with Autism Through a Self-management Treatment Package." *Journal of Applied Behavior Analysis* 23: 119–27.

Kohlberg, L. 1983. "Foreword to Promoting Moral Growth." In *Promoting Moral Growth,* J. Reimer, D. P. Paolitto, and R. R. Hersh. New York: Longman Press, ix-xvi.

Kohlenberg, R. J., and M. Tsai. 1987. "Functional Analytic Psychotherapy." In *Psychotherapists in Clinical Practice,* N. S. Jacobson, ed. New York: Guilford Press, 388–443.

Kurtz, P. 1973. *Humanist Manifestos I and II.* Buffalo, N.Y.: Prometheus Books.

Lamont, C. 1982. *The Philosophy of Humanism.* New York: Frederick Unger Publishing.

Leahey, T. H. 1987. *A History of Psychology,* 2nd ed. Englewood Cliffs, N.J.: Prentice-Hall.

Los Horcones. 1989. "Personalized Government: A Governmental System Based on Behavior Analysis." *Behavior Analysis and Social Action* 7: 42–47.

MacCorquodale, K. 1971. "Behaviorism is a Humanism." *The Humanist* 31(2): 11–12.

Madigan, T. 1988. "Misconceptions About Secular Humanism." *Free Inquiry* 8(4): 8.

Malcolm, J. G. 1986. "Treatment Choices and Informed Consent in Psychiatry: Implications of the Osheroff Case." *Journal of Psychiatry and Law,* Spring/Summer 1986: 9–108.

Malott, R. W. 1986. "Self-management, Rule-governed Behavior, and Everyday Life. In *Behavioral Science: Philosophical, Methodological, and Empirical Advances,* H. W. Reese and L. J. Parrott, eds. Hillsdale, N.J.: Lawrence Erlbaum, 207–28.

———. 1990. "Can We Build a World Free of Aversive Control?" *The ABA Newsletter,* Fall.

Marshall, E. 1988. "Flying Blind in the War on Drugs." *Science* 240: 1605–1607.

———. 1988a. "Drug Wars: Legalization Gets a Hearing." *Science* 241: 1157–59.

———. 1988b. "A War on Drugs with Real Troops?" *Science* 241: 13–15.

Marshall, J. 1987. "Drugs and United States Foreign Policy." In *Dealing with Drugs,* R. Hamowy, ed. Toronto: Lexington Books, 137–76.

Maslow, A. H. 1970. *Motivation and Personality.* New York: Harper and Row.

Matson, F. W. 1971. "Humanistic Theory: The Third Revolution in Psychology." *The Humanist* 31(2): 7–11.

McAuliffe, W. E., and R. A. Gordon. 1980. "Reinforcement and the Combination of Effects: Summary of a Theory of Opiate Addiction." In *Theories of Drug Abuse: Selected Contemporary Perspectives,* D. J. Lettieri, M. Sayers, and H. W. Pearson, eds. Rockville, Md.: National Institute on Drug Abuse.

McDowell, J. J. 1982. "The Importance of Herrnstein's Mathematical Statement of the Law of Effect for Behavior Therapy." *American Psychologist* 37: 771–79.

McFall, R. M. 1977. "Parameters of Self-monitoring." In *Behavioral Self-Management,* R. B. Stuart, ed. New York: Bruner/Mazel, 196–214.

Meyer, R. G., and P. Salmon. 1984. *Abnormal Psychology.* Boston: Allyn and Bacon, Inc.

Meyer, R. G., E. R. Landis, and J. R. Hays. 1988. *Law for the Psychotherapist.* New York: W. W. Norton.

Michaels, R. J. 1987. "The Market for Heroin Before and After

Legalization." In *Dealing with Drugs,* R. Hamowy, ed. Toronto: Lexington Books, 289–326.

Milleman, B. 1986. *And Two if by Sea: Fighting the Attack on America's Coasts.* Washington, D.C.: Coast Alliance, Inc.

Miller, L. K., and O. L. Miller. 1970. "Reinforcing Self-help Group Activities of Welfare Recipients." *Journal of Applied Behavior Analysis* 3: 57–64.

Miron, N. B. 1986. "Issues and Implications of Operant Conditioning." In *Taking sides: Clashing Views on Controversial Psychological Issues,* J. Rubinstein and B. D. Slife, eds. Guilford, Conn: Dushkin Group, 145–48.

Morris, E. K. 1984. "Public Information, Dissemination, and Behavior Analysis." *The Behavior Analyst* 8: 95–110.

Morrow, J. E. 1988. "Is Socialism Flawed?" *Behavior Analysis and Social Action* 6(2): 23–24.

Mowat, F. 1986. *Sea of Slaughter.* New York. Bantam Books.

Muck, T. C. 1988. "Stoned Logic." *Christianity Today* 32(18): 17.

Mumford, S. D. 1984. *American Democracy and the Vatican: Population Growth and National Security.* Amherst, N.Y.: The Humanist Press.

Murray, M. 1974. "The Treatment of Autism: A Human Protest." *The Journal of Humanistic Psychology* 14(2): 57–59.

Musto, D. F. 1987. "The History of Legislative Control over Opium, Cocaine, and Their Derivatives." In *Dealing with Drugs,* R. Hamowy, ed. Toronto: Lexington Books, 37–71.

Newman, B. 1989. "Psychotherapy and Science." *The Humanist* 49(1): 27, 28, 34.

———. 1991. *"A Clockwork Orange:* Burgess and Behavioral Interventions." *Behavior and Social Issues* 1(2): 61–70.

———. 1991. "Only Pragmatism Is Compatible with Behavior Analysis: A Reply to the Behaviorism and Socialism Debate." *Behavior and Social Issues* 1(2): 15–24.

———. 1991. "Behavior Analysis and the Drug Crisis." *Behavior and Social Issues* 1: 43–55.

———. 1992. "Telling Utopian from Dystopian Literature." Paper presented at the convention of the Association for Behavior Analysis, May 1992.

Nord, W. 1974. "Serendipity from Shaping the Shapers." *Journal of Humanistic Psychology* 14(4): 85–86.

O'Leary, K. D., and G. T. Wilson. 1987. *Behavior Therapy: Application and Outcome,* 2nd ed. Englewood Cliffs, N.J.: Prentice-Hall.

O'Leary, S. G., and D. R. Dubey. 1979. "Applications of Self-control Procedures by Children: A Review." *Journal of Applied Behavior Analysis* 12: 449–65.

Papanek, M. L. 1973. "How to Shape the Shapers." *Journal of Humanistic Psychology* 13(3): 55–58.

Paul, G. 1966. *Insight vs. Desensitization.* Stanford: Stanford University Press.

Pierce, J. P., P. Macaskill, Mappstat, and D. Hill. 1990. "Long-term Effectiveness of Mass Media Led Antismoking Campaigns in Australia." *American Journal of Public Health* 80: 565–69.

Rachlin, H., and L. Green. 1972. "Commitment, Choice, and Self-control." *Journal of the Experimental Analysis of Behavior* 17: 15–22.

Rakos, R. F. 1988a. "Capitalism, Socialism, and Behavioral Theory." *Behavior Analysis and Social Action* 6(2): 16–22.

———. 1988b. "Scientific Analysis or Political Ideology?" *Behavior Analysis and Social Action* 6(2): 32.

———. 1989. "Socialism, Behavioral Theory, and the Egalitarian Society." *Behavior Analysis and Social Action* 7: 23–29.

Randi, J. 1982. *Flim Flam!* Buffalo, N.Y.: Prometheus Books.

Richman, G. S., M. R. Riordan, M. L. Reiss, D. A. M. Pyles, and J. S. Bailey. 1988. "The Effects of Self-monitoring and Supervisor Feedback on Staff Performance in a Residential Setting." *Journal of Applied Behavior Analysis* 21: 401–409.

Robinson, D. N. 1988. *An Intellectual History of Psychology.* Madison, Wis.: University of Wisconsin Press.

Rogers, C. R. 1961. *On Becoming a Person.* Boston: Houghton Mifflin Company.

———. 1964. "Toward a Science of the Person." In *Behaviorism and Phenomenology,* T. W. Wann, ed. Chicago: The University of Chicago Press.

———. 1986. "Some Issues Concerning the Control of Human Behavior." In *Taking Sides: Clashing Views on Controversial Psychological Issues,* J. Rubinstein and B. Slife, eds. Guilford, Conn.: Dushkin Publishing Group, 366-76.

Rosenbaum, M. S., and R. S. Drabman. 1979. "Self-control Training in the Classroom: A Review and Critique." *Journal of Applied Behavior Analysis* 12: 467–85.

Rothbard, M. N. 1978. *For a New Liberty: The Libertarian Manifesto.* New York: The Libertarian Review Foundation.

Ryan, W. 1971. *Blaming the Victim.* New York: Vintage Books.

Sagan, C. 1987. "The Burden of Skepticism." *The Skeptical Inquirer* 12(1): 38–46.

Schreibman, L., and O. I. Lovaas. 1974. "Rejoinder to Murray's Article." *Journal of Humanistic Psychology* 14(2): 61–62.

Shanley, D. A. 1988. "Reaching Our Nation's Dropouts." *Youth Policy* 10(7): 25–29.

Sheaffer, R. 1989. "Socialism Is Incompatible with Humanism." *Free Inquiry* 9(4): 19–20.

Sidman, M. 1989. *Coercion and Its Fallout.* Boston: Authors Cooperative, Inc.

Skinner, B. F. 1953. *Science and Human Behavior.* New York: The Free Press.

———. 1971a. *Beyond Freedom and Dignity.* New York: Bantam Books.

———. 1971b. "Humanistic Behaviorism." *The Humanist* 31(3): 35.

———. 1972. "Humanism and Behaviorism." *The Humanist* 32(4): 18–20.

———. 1974. *About Behaviorism.* New York: Random House.

———. 1976. "The Ethics of Helping People." *The Humanist* 36(1): 7–11.

———. 1982a. "Freedom and the Control of Men." In *Skinner for the Classroom,* R. Epstein, ed. Champaign, Ill.: Research Press, 135–52.

———. 1982b. "B. F. Skinner: An Autobiography." In *Skinner for the Classroom,* R. Epstein, ed. Champaign, Ill.: Research Press, 9–38.

———. 1986. "Some Issues Concerning the Control of Human Behavior." In *Taking Sides: Clashing Views on Controversial Psychological Issues,* J. Rubinstein and B. Slife, eds. Guilford, Conn: Dushkin Publishing Group, 358–65.

———. 1989. *Recent Issues in the Analysis of Behavior.* Toronto, Canada: Merrill Publishing.

Sobell, M. B., and L. C. Sobell. 1984. "The Aftermath of Heresy:

A Response to Pendery et al.'s (1982) Critique of 'Individualized Behavior Therapy for alcoholics.' " *Behaviour Research and Therapy* 22: 413–40.

Stagner, R. 1988. *A History of Psychological Theories.* New York: Macmillan Publishing Company.

Stokes, T. F., and S. B. Fawcett. 1977. "Evaluating Municipal Policy: An Analysis of a Refuse-Packaging Program. *Journal of Applied Behavior Analysis* 10: 391–98.

Stone, K., and J. R. Thompson. 1989. "Drug Testing: A National Controversy." *Journal of Alcohol and Drug Education* 34(3): 70–79.

Sutker, P. B., and R. P. Archer. 1984. "Opiate Abuse and Dependence Disorders." In *Comprehensive Handbook of Psychopathology,* H. E. Adams and P. B. Sutker, eds. New York: Plenum Press, 585–621.

Swell, L. 1974. *Enhancing the Self: Techniques for Teachers.* Privately published, no place of publication noted.

Szasz, T. 1987. "The Morality of Drug Controls." In *Dealing with Drugs,* R. Hamowy, ed. Toronto: Lexington Books, 327–51.

Tobacyk, J. J. 1983. "Reduction in Paranormal Belief Among Participants in a College Course." *The Skeptical Inquirer* 8(1): 57–61.

Todd, J. T. 1990. "The Great Power of Steady Misrepresentation." Paper presented at the convention of the Association for Behavior Analysis, Nashville, May 1990.

Torisky, C. V. 1990. "In Memoriam—Some Final Thoughts on Bruno Bettelheim." *The Advocate* 22(3 and 4): 12.

Trebach, A. S. 1987. "The Need for Reform of International Narcotics Laws." In *Dealing with Drugs,* R. Hamowy, ed. Toronto: Lexington Books, 103–36.

Ulman, J. 1988. "Just Say No to Commodity Fetishism: A Reply to Rakos." *Behavior Analysis and Social Action* 6(2): 25–31.

———. 1989. "Beyond the Carrot and the Stick: A Behavioral Rejoinder to Rakos." *Behavior Analysis and Social Action* 7: 30–34.

Van Houten, R., S. Axelrod, J. S. Bailey, J. E. Favell, R. M. Foxx, B. A. Iwata, and O. I. Lovaas. 1988. "The Right to Effective Behavioral Treatment." *Journal of Applied Behavior Analysis* 21: 381–84.

Van Houten, R., E. Morrison, R. Jarvis, and M. McDonald. 1974. "The Effects of Explicit Timing and Feedback on Compositional Response Rate in Elementary School Children." *Journal of Applied Behavior Analysis* 7: 547–55.

Vargas, E. A. 1988. "Teachers in the Classroom: Behaviorological Science and an Effective Instructional Technology." *Youth Policy* 10(7): 33–36.

Wahler, R. G., and J. J. Fox. 1981. "Setting Events in Applied Behavior Analysis: Toward a Conceptual and Methodological Expansion." *Journal of Applied Behavior Analysis* 14: 327–38.

Watkins, C. L. 1988. "Project Follow-Through: A Story of the Identification and Neglect of Effective Instruction." *Youth Policy* 10(7): 7–11.

Watson, J .B. 1970. *Behaviorism.* New York: W. W. Norton.

Whitlock, F. A. 1987. "Addiction." In *The Oxford Companion to the Mind,* R. L. Gregory, ed. New York: Oxford University Press, 3–5.

Wilson, G. T., and K. D. O'Leary. 1980. *Principles of Behavior Therapy.* Englewood Cliffs, N.J.: Prentice-Hall.

Wine, S. T. 1985. *Judaism Beyond God.* Farmington Hills, Mich.: Society for Humanistic Judaism.

Woods, J. H. 1978. "Behavioral Pharmacology of Drug Self-administration." In *Psychopharmacology: A Generation of Progress,* M. A. Lipton, A. DiMascio, and K. F. Killam, eds. New York: Raven Press, 595–607.

Woods, P. J. 1984. "Evidence for the Effectiveness of a Reading Program in Changing Beliefs in the Paranormal." *The Skeptical Inquirer* 9(1): 67–70.

Woolfolk, R. L., and F. C. Richardson. 1984. "Behavior Therapy and the Ideology of Modernity." *American Psychologist* 39: 777–86.

Wyatt, J. W. 1990. "U.S. Students Fare Poorly, Feel Better about Themselves, Study Shows." *Behavior Analysis Digest* 2(1): 4.

Zinberg, N. E. 1987. "The Use and Misuse of Intoxicants: Factors in the Development of Controlled Use." In *Dealing with Drugs,* R. Hamowy, ed. Toronto: Lexington Books, 247–79.